Anonymous

History of charity organization in the United States; Report

Anonymous

History of charity organization in the United States; Report

ISBN/EAN: 9783337723712

Printed in Europe, USA, Canada, Australia, Japan

Cover: Foto ©ninafisch / pixelio.de

More available books at **www.hansebooks.com**

No. 61   Ncv. '93

Charity Organization Society

OF THE CITY OF NEW YORK

HISTORY

OF

CHARITY ORGANIZATION

IN THE

UNITED STATES

REPORT OF COMMITTEE OF NATIONAL CONFERENCE OF CHARITIES AND CORRECTION,

CHARLES D. KELLOGG, *Chairman*

CHICAGO

1893

BOSTON
PRESS OF GEO. H. ELLIS, 141 FRANKLIN STREET
1894

CHARITY ORGANIZATION IN THE UNITED STATES.

REPORT OF THE COMMITTEE ON HISTORY OF CHARITY ORGANIZATION.

BY CHARLES D. KELLOGG, CHAIRMAN.

Under more than a score of names there may be enumerated ninety-two associations in the United States and the Dominion of Canada as in existence in 1893, which profess loyalty to the principles characteristic of the movement known as the Organization of Charity. Of these the greatest variation of names arises among the twenty societies originally inaugurated as Relief Societies but which have adopted in part the methods of Charity Organization Societies or Associated Charities after their formation, and which are in correspondence with them (Appendix A). Of the whole number sixty-five (65) have made returns, with widely varying precision and completeness, to the Committee on the History of Charity Organization of this Twentieth Annual Conference of Charities and Correction, and upon these returns this report is based.

HISTORY.

CONDITIONS TWENTY YEARS AGO.—Twenty years ago, in the sense of an agency for bringing charitable and municipal relief organizations into concert of action, there were no Charity Organization Societies in America. There were in many cities voluntary general relief societies professedly ready to undertake any sort of humane task within their ability. In some instances, they laid claim to most approved maxims of work, such as raising the dependent poor into independence, the need of investigation as a basis of relief, the duty of repressing imposture. Rarely they employed the Friendly Visitor, and made employment the basis of relief. But, as they were invariably distributors of material aid, this function submerged all others, and they sank into the sea of common almsgiving, appealing to their patrons for support on the ground that the money given to them would enable them to enlarge the number of their beneficiaries or increase the amount of their gifts, and attracting the needy to their doors with the hope of loaves and fishes. In many quarters there was no lack of judicious reasoning, or of admission that the moral nature and the social lot of the poor were large factors in the problem of pauperism; but the efforts to extirpate it were feeble and incidental, not dominant. On every side the current of public sentiment was that every penny spent in administration was so much abstracted from the poor, and that the best management was that which entailed the least cost in getting bread and soup to the hungry, and shelter, fuel, and clothing to the cold. Even in religious missions to the extremely depressed it was felt that a man should not be called upon to hear the gospel in rags or on an empty stomach, and their dismal chapels were largely frequented by sordid dissemblers who conformed for gain, and shunned by those in whom a large measure of self-respect still prevailed.

RELIEF TWENTY YEARS AGO.—Legal relief consisted of outdoor and indoor systems, the latter being universally institutional; and therefore it only falls incidentally within the scope of Charity Organization efforts. The practice of legal outdoor relief differed greatly in different communities. In New York City the provision for this form of aid was comparatively slight, and consisted in appropriations for fuel distribution and for the adult blind in equally inadequate amounts, and a trifling sum for medicines at the City Hospital. In some cities, like Buffalo, Philadelphia and Brooklyn, large appropriations of money were made for outdoor relief, and its administration did not escape the suspicion of corrupt and political taint at times. In New England cities and towns, overseers of the poor or selectmen distributed, much at their caprice, the relief provided by taxation. But from every quarter testimony arises that the system was without adequate safeguards of investigation, tests of destitution, or means of hindering duplication of relief from several sources simultaneously, or of making the relief adequate to the necessity. Private almsgiving, for the most part through organized and often incorporated societies, was profuse and chaotic, while still behind the demands made upon it, and was dispersed in tantalizing doles miserably inadequate for effectual succor where the need was genuine, and dealt out broadcast among the clamorous and impudent. Amid all this mean prodigality there were almoners seriously and studiously in earnest to make the relief they gave beneficent and not injurious; but the system, or rather want of it, and the exaggerated conceptions of their resources excited among the poor, degraded and impeded their labors. In fact, twenty years ago those in the United States who thought that the function of relief could be lifted above temporary material aid were few in number and but just beginning to be heard. Indeed, it was the industrial depression following the commercial crisis which began in the autumn of 1873, throwing multitudes out of work and making a heavy draft upon the benevolent, which seems to afford the starting-point for the examination and reformation of the prevailing methods of charity.

BEGINNINGS. -In 1872 the nearest approximation to Charity Organization to be found in the United States was the Chardon Street Building in Boston. It was erected in 1869 by joint contributions from the city and personal subscribers, in pursuance of a plan first promulgated by Hon. Robert C. Winthrop in 1857, and subsequently advocated in the annual reports of the Boston Provident Association, of which he was the president. Under its roof are the offices of the official boards and the principal voluntary relief societies of the city. The economy and advantages of proximity for the purpose of exchanging information and concerting measures of dealing with applicants for help had been clearly pointed out, and the existence of this building facilitated the subsequent systematic development of registration and co-operation in that city.

GERMANTOWN. -Although the movement to organize charities in the cities of the United States everywhere traces its origin to the London Society and its publications, or to the discussions which arose concerning it, there were several independent centres in which it appeared nearly simultaneously in this country. In 1874 Rev. Charles G. Ames led in the formation, upon London models, in Germantown, a suburban ward of Philadelphia, of an association which employed household visitors to investigate applicants for aid, availed itself of the soup-house, fuel societies, churches, and especially of the outdoor municipal relief in procuring the requisite assistance, and supplemented it as need indicated from its own resources. It brought the charitable operations of Germantown into unexpected unison ; repressed imposture and the artificial appetite for aid of such poor as sought it only because they wanted to share in the good things provided for those who asked, and not because they would otherwise be destitute of them ; reformed outdoor municipal relief ; discovered real cases of hardship ; and gained the confidence of the benevolent of all denominations in that community. This association profoundly influenced the measures adopted by the larger society formed in Philadelphia a few years later.

EARLY INVESTIGATIONS. — In the same year a Bureau of Charities was formed in New York City, of which Mr. Henry E. Pellew was chief promoter and secretary, that proposed to register persons receiving outdoor relief, either from the city, benevolent societies, or individuals ; but the scheme was frustrated the next year by the refusal of the largest relief-giving society in the city to co-operate. This plan met with better success in Boston. In the autumn of 1875 the Co-operative Society of Visitors among the Poor was formed in Boston, whose theatre of operation was in the North End. The plan was a modification of the Elberfeld system as proposed by Octavia Hill for London. No visitor was to have more than four "cases " on hand, and lists were obtained from a physician who was the visitor for the Provident Association in that congested and poor district. The society held weekly conferences of visitors and representatives of other charities, and it opened a work-room in the Chardon Street Charity Building.

BUFFALO.-- Buffalo has the honor of being the first city in the United States to produce a complete Charity Organization Society of the London type. The Rev. S. H. Gurteen, an English clergyman, who had been active in the London Society. was settled as an assistant minister in St. Paul's Church there ; and he systematized the work of his parish guild so that every application for aid was promptly investigated. He proposed in 1877 the creation of a clearing-office to which the charitable agencies of the city should send daily reports ; and he lectured on " Phases of Charity," attracting much attention. Simultaneously citizens, having met in conference. were engaged in an effort to reform the methods of municipal outdoor relief, which had become extravagant, was careless and corrupt. Failing to obtain legislation in Albany to create a commission for its

control, they secured an ordinance from the city, under which, in
October, 1877, all applications for relief were for the first time
investigated by the police. On Dec. 11, 1877, as a result of
these agitations, the Charity Organization Society was set afoot
at a public meeting; and it adhered to the principle of co-ordinating
existing relief agencies and giving no relief from its own funds except
in rare emergencies.

NEW HAVEN.— New Haven was next in line, May 23, 1878, with
the co-operation of the older local relief societies, and took charge
of cases until investigation elicited some mode of making more permanent disposition of them.

BOSTON.— In the spring of 1876 a Registration Committee was
formed by private citizens of Boston, and work was begun in the
autumn, carried on until the spring of 1878. and then abandoned in
view of the larger enterprise then under discussion.   It had demon-
strated the value of reports from the offices of the Overseers of the
Poor, of benevolent societies, and of the Friendly Visitors above referred to, when collated; but it had failed to obtain the entire co-operation of relief organizations.   Much discussion and many conferences
ensued during that year, looking to the formation of a society upon
the principles of Charity Organization, which would bring into association all the relief agencies, ecclesiastical and secular, of the city. '
The large relief societies knew the worth of registration, but doubted
the value of "friendly visiting."   They were willing to support the
new movement, provided "the visitors had no power of relief."
This condition was fortunately acceded to; and on Feb. 26, 1879,
a provisional commission was formed by delegates from many charities, which carried on the work until December 8, when the present
constitution of the Associated Charities of Boston was adopted,
and went into effect.

PHILADELPHIA.— Philadelphia brought forward its type in 1878.
In the previous autumn the officers of several soup societies, dissatis-
fied with the results of their previous work, called a public meeting
of citizens to confer upon larger and better methods for the future.
A large committee was appointed to draw up a plan; and on June
13, 1878, a constitution was adopted and a provisional organization
set on foot.   This instrument was dominated by the idea of repro-
ducing in each of the thirty wards of the city a complete association,
like that existing in Germantown.   The Central Board was to be com-

posed of two delegates from each ward, which should meet monthly; and meanwhile its powers were to be exercised by an Executive Committee. ' The provisional commission proceeded to organize Ward Associations with great rapidity, and in due time delegates were chosen to the Central Board and the Society was organized under its constitution. The immediate results of so cumbrous and democratic a scheme was that twenty-three societies were formed in as many wards or groups of contiguous wards, pledged to take care of all the distress and penury each in its territorial limits. Each raised its own funds, and disbursed them without control; and, as there were but few persons in them who understood Charity Organization principles, the work often fell into wrong hands, and the Ward Associations were so many new almsgiving societies. By their attitude they were virtually saying to all the older charitable societies that there was no need of them, and they, as a rule, refused co-operation, and still withhold it. Another result was that the Central Board had no authority to control the methods of relief, and was itself subordinate to its ward constituencies. One hundred and eighty persons were needed to fill the offices of directors, while there were large corps of visitors having a semi-independent organization. The movement was highly popular at the start, and came in the first year into an income of nearly $40,000. It offered itself to the community as a complete, independent, and self-contained system for dealing with every phase of charity; but its very sufficiency obscured the vital fact that Charity Organization aims at no more independence than is necessary to maintain existence, and should be subservient to all existing charity agencies with a view to their co-ordination. Great reliance for the uniform working of the system was placed upon monthly conferences of all the workers, directors, local superintendents, and visitors, and for a time these conferences were well attended and were highly educational. In due time the plan was revised, the choice of the Central Board was transferred from the Ward Associations to the annual meeting of the general society, its initiative and oversight was strengthened, and the wards were consolidated into eighteen districts; but the original features had made a deep impression which has not been obliterated. The business of registration and co-operation sank into control of the district organizations; the Central office drifted into the specialty of caring for non-residents and wayfarers' lodges; and the society remains as it started out to be, a relief agency with Charity Organization tradtions. //

NEWPORT.— The benevolent community of Newport was aroused in 1878 to the need of better co-operation among its charities by a realization that a large proportion of the population of that prosperous and wealthy town was, through the enormous increase of public and private almsgiving, being rapidly pauperized. A study of the situation revealed the astonishing fact that "one in ten of the population was either wholly or in part supported by charity, and that nearly one-half of that charity was thrown away." As the best remedy for meeting the growing evil, the Charity Organization Society was formed Feb. 12, 1879. None of our societies have continuously done more intelligent and successful work, and but few have accomplished equal results in uplifting the families under their care. The marked feature in its history is its success in cultivating habits of thrift and of saving among its beneficiaries.

CINCINNATI.— Cincinnati was promptly in the field Nov. 18, 1879. The Associated Charities was initiated through influences aroused chiefly by the Women's Christian Association and other societies, the inaugural meeting being held the same hour with the first annual meeting of the Philadelphia society, and reciprocal congratulations being exchanged between them. It started avowedly on the lines laid down in the Boston society, but practically it fell into the Philadelphia methods, and created or adopted twelve district organizations dispensing relief and which the Central Board was not able to control. Fortunately, the tact and force of the General Secretary repressed much of the mischief, secured a general registration, and gave cohesion to the system until 1886, when he resigned and the society lapsed into a relief agency, became unpopular, and was about to be abandoned; when in 1889 it was reorganized, the district treasuries were absorbed into one, the central authority made dominant, and the distribution of relief was stopped, to the great increase of efficiency and public confidence.

BROOKLYN.— Brooklyn was another centre where the movement arose spontaneously. In 1877 a commission of citizens undertook the investigation of outdoor relief, which in that year comprised 46,350 beneficiaries and involved an expenditure of $141,207. This resulted in restricting municipal outdoor relief to coal in 1878, and in its total abolition the next year. In 1879 Mr. Seth Low, who had been providentially and unpremeditatedly present at the inauguration of the Buffalo society and deeply impressed thereby, enlisted Mr. Alfred T. White; and they, with others who had been instrumental in abolishing the outdoor relief of the city, together with the volunteer visitors of the outdoor poor, organized the Brooklyn Bureau of Charities, which does not give relief, but maintains wood-yards, laundries, work-rooms, and a woman's lodging-house.

INDIANAPOLIS.— Indianapolis enjoyed the labors of Rev. Oscar C. McCulloch as president of the Benevolent Society, in which office he had made careful studies of the poor-relief problem. In 1876 Mr. King, the Township Trustee or Overseer of the Poor, began to systematize and improve the administration of poor-relief, and together these gentlemen led on to the formation, Dec. 5, 1879, of the Charity Organization Society.

NEW YORK.— New York, as the largest centre of population in the country, demands notice here. The difficulties encountered in securing influential co-operation in 1874 for a time paralyzed further effort, although the necessity for some organization was long discussed by persons interested in charitable enterprises. In 1881 the matter was taken up by the State Board of Charities, and through its initiative the Charity Organization Society of the City of New York was founded in January, 1882, and incorporated on the 10th of May following. It followed the Boston plan in respect to the important features of giving no relief and of creating district associations maintained from a common treasury and under central control.

NATIONAL CONFERENCE.— All other Charity Organization Societies in the United States trace their origin to these now enumerated, which have been selected not only as among the earliest in the field, but as illustrating the diversity of origin of the movement, the causes which immediately led to the associations for organizing charity, and the two types of societies, those which combine relief from their own funds with their methods and those which do not. The movement found an expression of its unity in the National Conference of Charities and Correction, which is itself an outgrowth of the American Social Science Association. It is first mentioned in the proceedings of the Chicago Conference of 1879, where Mr. Seth Low presented a description of the work in Brooklyn, and a committee was formed to report upon Charity Organization. Two years later, at Boston. nineteen societies reported to the National Conference; and the committee grew to a Section, which published a separate report of its own proceedings.

SUPPRESSION OF OUTDOOR RELIEF.--Simultaneously with the beginning of Charity Organization, and promoted by the same men, there was a repression in important cities of official outdoor relief. Returns from four cities for that time give the following results : —

City.	Year.	Out-relief.	Year.	Out-relief
Brooklyn	1877	$141,207	1880	None.
Buffalo	1877	99,196	1880	$37,868
Indianapolis, Centre Township	1876	90,000	1880	8,000
Philadelphia	1879	66,000	1880	None.
Amount saved to tax-payers				350,535
Total		$396,403		$396,403

While this elimination of outdoor relief was not pressed by formal action of our societies, Charity Organizationists claimed the credit of it as the result of their agitation and personal effort, and it was exactly in the line of the principles they advocated. Diligent inquiry showed that no suffering ensued in consequence of the withdrawal, while the admissions to almshouses and infirmaries in the cities named contemporaneously decreased. This event attracted wide attention in watchful official circles, evinced the value of the investigations which preceded it, and disclosed the worse than useless prodigality of outdoor relief. Its influence spread far and wide beyond the limits where it could be statistically followed. and was the beginning of a wiser administration of the charitable funds raised by taxation in many communities.

TEN YEARS OF GROWTH.— In 1882 there were twenty-two Charity Organization Societies known to exist in the United States, and ten others which had adopted some of the leading features of this movement, and were enrolled as correspondents with the former societies. They embraced cities and towns having a population of 6,331,700, or twelve per cent. of the total of the United States ; and among them were the chief centres of influence in the country. Of these societies ten were in or had just completed the first year of their operations; and among them were some destined to be the most important in the Union, administering in incorporated populations of

2,363.138. From this point it is practicable to make tables and comparisons which exhibit the growth, mode of operations, and results of the Charity Organization movement for a decade in the United States. (See Appendix B.)

At the close of the year 1892 there were ninety-two Charity Organization and affiliated societies, — an increase of two hundred and seventy-eight per cent. in ten years; and they were located in cities and towns comprising a population estimated at 11,080,766 (by census of 1890, 10,419,150). Of these, six were founded in 1883, nine in 1884, five in 1885, four in 1886, two in 1887, six in 1888, six in 1889, six in 1890, four in 1891, and five in 1892. Of these, thirty-two report that their organizations sprang up independently of other charitable societies: fifteen, that they were promoted by existing charities; six, that they were reorganizations; one, that it was a consolidation of two movements; and one, that it was the enlargement of a committee to investigate outdoor poor relief. In nearly every instance the motive leading to these organizations is declared to have been discontent with the prodigality and inefficiency of public relief, and the chaotic state of private charity. Twenty-two of our associations report that voluntary charity was lavish, uninformed, and aimless, with no concert of action; two, that it was variable, and therefore unreliable; one, that it was impeded by discouragement; and one, that it did not exist in the community.

Two Types.— Classified by their relation to almsgiving, twenty-five of our associations report that they do not give material relief from their own funds: twenty, that they do relieve: nine, that they do so only in emergent cases, of which two add that they do so in order to avoid official outdoor relief. Thus two classes are formed, one of which comprises almsgiving agencies in which thirty societies enroll themselves, and the other relies upon other societies and upon individuals for the physical resources it recommends, and thus secures relief by co-operation; and in this class twenty-five societies enroll themselves. Of the twenty relief-giving societies, six are affiliated or are older organizations readjusted. Omitting these, we find that fifty-one per cent. of those reporting to us do not directly relieve, while forty-nine per cent. do. In 1881 there were but twelve relieving and seven non-relieving societies reporting,— a percentage of sixty-three to the former and thirty-seven to the latter. These are instructive figures, showing the tendency of the movement, when its principles are faithfully followed, toward the type of a pure organization agency as the complement of the other charitable enterprises of society. (See Appendix C.)

PROPAGANDA. — The methods taken to disseminate Charity Organization principles are various. Most of the societies publish annual reports, though a few of the smaller ones publish nothing. In a few instances, monthly reports are published. There are thirteen societies which rely for the promulgation of their views solely upon personal advocacy and the results of their work: twenty make use of local papers, one of them maintaining a weekly column in a local newspaper; sixteen issue occasional papers, tracts, and pamphlets; four publish periodicals; and several make use of public conferences, lectures, and meetings. There are also in several cities Directories of Charities, describing the benevolent institutions and associations therein, which are prepared by Charity Organization Societies.

LAPSED SOCIETIES.— It is known to this committee that thirteen Charity Organization Societies have been formed and dissolved. They were located as follows, the dates of their organization being also given as far as ascertained : —

——.	Altoona, Pa.	1884.	Paterson, N.J.
1882.	Chicago. Merged in a relief society.	1881.	Princeton, N.J.
1886.	Columbus, Ohio.	1885.	Quincy, Ill.
1886.	Dedham, Mass.	1884.	Sandusky, Ohio.
1883.	District of Columbia. Suspended.	1888.	St. Joseph, Mo.
1881.	Lowell, Mass.	1890.	Toledo, Ohio.
1883.	Moline, Ill.		

There are twenty-five societies enrolled which have made no report, of which six are on the affiliated or readjusted list. Some of these preserve an organization as a nucleus for rebuilding, and some are the chief relieving agencies of the communities in which they are located. A few are practically in suspension. Various causes may be assigned for the creation of this delinquent and lapsed list. For the most part it embraces comparatively small communities, where the field for combining benevolent enterprises is small, and in some cases the management of poor-relief is fairly good and easily influenced. There are instances where the Charity Organization Society was the first and only general non-sectarian association in the town, and it drifted into the work of relief. More frequently the nascent society yielded to the opposition of the friends of the old system, or was planted in a community not prepared to comprehend and maintain it, or it lacked the superintendency essential to the promotion of a reform so radical and complex as that involved in the readjustment of the benevolence of a whole community. Probably the lack of trained and capable superintendents, and of suitable Friendly Visitors prepared to bear the restraints of Charity Organization, is the chief cause of miscarriage: for where a society has been able to command these, and to put them in control of its work, it has taken root and won support to its standards.

ON REPORTS FROM SOCIETIES.— The last ten years of the history of Charity Organization this report will exhibit in tabulated statistics appended thereto, merely calling attention here to their salient points and results. For its preparation a circular letter was prepared (see Appendix D), and sent to every society know to your committee. It is to be regretted that many of the returns were so imperfect as to render them useless for purposes of comparison or for illustrating the growth of the movement. In some instances, the society had kept no records which would supply the information sought; in others, the correspondent misconceived the object of the question, and replied in general terms instead of statistics; and in still others there was little appreciation of the importance of this occasion or the value of full and accurate reports. On the other hand, many of the returns bear evidence of excellent office records, systematic work, and painstaking to fill the blanks in the circular fully and accurately. A study of the appendices to this report will disclose the imperfections referred to. From the material furnished the following exhibit is made.

CHANGES OF METHOD. *Relief Adopted.*— In a movement of so recent origin there has been but small room to judge of the effects of various methods and to devise new plans of work. Most of the Charity Organization Societies still adhere to the methods with which they started out. Still there are three distinct phases of development to be detected in the growth of their work: (1) the adoption of material relief: (2) the abolition or reduction of such relief; and (3) the expansion of Friendly Visiting and provident enterprises. Four societies report a change from organizing and co-operative work by adding thereto the distribution of some form of alms. Worcester at first created a separate treasury known as the Fund of Benevolent Individuals, on which its officers drew for cases of necessity : and thus it began with keeping its organization and visiting work apart from the distribution of alms. But the expedient was cumbersome, and this fund was absorbed into the general treasury, and thence distributed as the need of applicants required. At the same time this relief work is a matter of regret, and the reason assigned for its continuance is the small number and inadequacy of charity societies in that city. In Rochester, under the form of " Immediate Relief," our society has entered on a phase of general almsgiving, probably as a temporary makeshift until some more effectual disposition can be made of cases in its care. But the report is made that this change has greatly conciliated public opinion, and increased the contributions to the treasury of the society. The Lynn society became trustee of a bequest for the benefit of local poor, and turned the income into a loan and emergency fund ; while Minneapolis established an emergency fund, but, restricting its use to its paid agents, kept its Friendly Visiting corps free from being entangled with its distribution. From these statements the inference is that alms relief has been for the most part taken up in a very restricted way, and but few Charity Organization Societies which did not begin with it have since adopted it.

Relief Withheld.— On the other hand, several of our societies have distinctly receded from the work of material relief, to seek it by co-operation with other benevolent agencies. Notable is the history of Cincinnati, the experience of which in coquetting with relief distribution from its own treasury is already recited above, and which in consequence came near the verge of extinction. Now, freed from that alliance, it is one of the most effective societies upon the list. A like experiment went on in Detroit. Its funds were withdrawn from distribution among the poor, its too independent district associations were abolished, and a board of fifteen trustees was put in complete charge of the administration. From the important city of Philadelphia, where the society began with its sovereignty lodged in ward associations, that system still nominally remains ; but the report comes that the Central Board has gained in influence and authority over the ward administrations, and is now enforcing the charity organization theory more vigorously than was possible at first. In Pueblo and San Francisco direct relief work has receded, and been replaced with better systems of investigation and co-operation with other charitable agencies. Syracuse has restricted its material relief to the merest tiding over, through co-operating agencies, of emergent cases until some judgment can be reached on the better disposition of an applicant for aid, and this society enrolls itself as a non-relieving association. In Orange, N.J., and Seattle, Wash., the employment of a paid and expert superintendent has been found to put an end to feebleness and inefficiency.

DEVELOPMENT.-- It is interesting to note the lines of development of agencies which the Charity Organization Societies keep in their own control. The influence they have had in promoting beneficent schemes to be carried on by others will be touched upon in later paragraphs. The developments here referred to are those which have been engrafted on our societies after their foundation and as a result of experience. But the inference must not be drawn that they are peculiar to the societies enumerated. Many others began their career with Friendly Visitors, employment agencies, registration, investigation, and provident schemes, and where these features are here enumerated they simply show the tendency of all societies to come into line in the nature of their work. Baltimore has added an employment bureau and friendly visiting to its original plan ; so also has Brooklyn, while also developing labor tests of real need ; Bangor has improved its system of registration and investigation ; New Haven indexes in book records its card registration, has adopted friendly visiting, and established a savings fund ; New York has learned to make its exchanges of information more prompt and complete, has created a provident savings fund, and encouraged provident schemes and labor tests ; Waterbury has added provident schemes ; and Wilmington, Del., has sought larger conformity to the work of the greater sister societies.

FINANCE.-- In extenuation of the enormous percentages of contributing support, which otherwise would seem extravagant, it must be remembered that this review embraces only fourteen organizations in 1882, several of which were in their first year, and compares them with fifty-four societies reporting ten years later. This in itself represents an increase of nearly three hundred per cent. in the number of organizations participating in this report ; and the other growths are closely correspondent. Thus in the last ten years the number of individual contributors quadrupled, the number of contributing churches and societies increased more than three hundred and seven per cent., while nine societies received aid from State and municipal treasuries to the extent of $17,878 in 1892, and another an office free of rent. The income of forty-eight societies increased threefold in 1892 over that of seventeen in 1882, and reached an aggregate of $263,421. Fourteen societies report the beginning of invested funds, and together they held property and securities valued at $409,038. (See Appendix E.)

REAL ESTATE.—The real estate which has passed into possession of Charity Organization Societies demands attention not only for its magnitude, but as indicative of the permanency of this sort of work among the established features of modern social life. These endowments began in Buffalo, 1880, when, through the generosity of a single individual, the Fitch Crèche was established at a cost of about $40,-000, an institution which has done much to promote industry and thrift among the poor, and is the best equipped agency of the kind in America. To this gift Mr. Benjamin Fitch added much other property, conveying it by deed of trust to the society for the purpose of encouraging provident schemes. The Fitch Institute, completed in 1883, not only affords offices for the accommodation of the society, but within it are comprised an Accident Hospital and a Training School for nursery maids and domestic servants. These properties form the greater part of the $300,000 invested on behalf of the Buffalo society. Very noble is the admirable and imposing United Charities Building of New York, erected by Mr. John S. Kennedy, and dedicated March 6, 1893. It was deeded to four of the principal charity societies of the city, who manage it through a board of trustees chosen by them. Each has an equal share in the use and income of the structure, and one of these is the Charity Organization Society. As it cost over $600,000, the equity of this society is valued at $150,000. The Charities Building in Chardon Street, Boston, was already in existence when the Associated Charities of that city were organized; and here that society has always had its headquarters free of rent. It was built in part by private subscriptions. The Bridgeport society owns a building valued at $11,000, that of Cleveland one valued at $23,000, and New Haven has a fund of $30,000 dedicated to a like purpose. These edifices are centres of conference, co-operation, and exchanges of information, and virtually add an estimated value of about $220,000 to the invested resources of Charity Organization in the United States, making a total of $530,000.

INTERNAL ORGANIZATION.—With pardonable pride attention is called to the fact that fifty-two societies report placing in the field of administration and personal service of the needy in 1892 an army of 5,476 men and women. This number is below the actual fact, since seventeen of the societies make no return of their administrative officers, and eight none of their Friendly Visitors, while Philadelphia fails to enumerate the officers and visitors of its eighteen large district societies with which several hundred visitors are connected. The total number is doubtless over 6,000. This report would gladly exhibit the relative part taken by men and by women in this work; but its conclusions are marred by the fact that six societies have not distinguished the sexes in their returns, and these embrace some important cities. Where no distinction has been made, administrative offices have been credited to men, who predominate therein, and for a like reason visitors have been reckoned as women in our tables; and the results as stated are the best now attainable. In administrative work 763 men, an increase of 157 per cent. in ten years, and 511 women, an increase of 220 per cent., were engaged in 1892. Of paid officials the same year there were 77 men (increase 220 per cent.) and 135 women (increase 250 per cent.) in the service; while of Friendly Visitors 456 men (increase 1,400 per cent.) and 3,534 women (increase 165 per cent.) toiled in the homes or over the ill-fortunes of applicants for aid. As 74,704 cases came under the notice of the societies, this would give an average of 17.6 cases to each visitor,—a number altogether too large for effective work. Boston has developed friendly visiting to the highest efficiency, having 767 visitors in the field. There this feature of the work is regarded as "the soul of the movement," and there was in 1892 one visitor to each 1.98 cases treated. Indeed, here the Charity Organization movement grew out of a Friendly Visitors' Association. Brooklyn comes next on the list, having 532 visitors, and yet, in common with New York, feels its work hampered and restricted by the lack of an efficient force of visitors. Cincinnati regards this as the most successful feature of its work; and from many quarters comes the expression of a desire to enlarge this department. It is the means by which the higher resources of society, its hope, discipline, thrift, and kindness of heart, are diffused among the depressed and those who have fallen by the way; it is the means of contact with poverty of mind and purse; it is the vital agency in evoking the capacities of the poor for self-maintenance. If Charity Organization seeks to withdraw that material relief which weakens independence, it does so in order to replace it with the choicer and holier aid of wisdom, self-control, and sympathy. (See Appendix F.) Fifteen societies control one hundred subordinate district conferences or associations, and twenty-nine avail themselves of conferences among officers and visitors to consider methods and the disposition to be made of individual and family cases. These conferences range from weekly through monthly and quarterly sessions. A notable example of kindred work lasted through the first eight years of the Philadelphia society. Here once a month an Assembly of the whole society was held and numerously attended, at which papers were read, and practical discussions maintained on the problems of charity; and the effect of them was incalculable in educating the workers and even the community in a sense of responsibility for their poor brothers and sisters. It was a popular school for teaching charity, and did much to plant the principles of Charity Organization in the confidence of the public and to unify the work of the large and too independent Ward Associations.

LINES OF WORK DEVELOPED. (See Appendix G.) *Repression of Public Outdoor Relief.*— Outdoor relief from tax-rates was long obnoxious to the students of the English poor-law system; and Parliament vainly tried to abolish it by confining aid to the workhouse, which was thus intended to be a test of destitution. But the laws broke down, and the vicious distribution by parish officers still went on. Together with much that is beyond criticism in common law, the evils of this system were imported from the mother country, and were widely applied in the United States. One of the first movements on Charity Organization lines was, consequently, a widely diffused effort to reform or abolish municipal outdoor relief. In some instances, as in Brooklyn and to some extent in Buffalo, it antedated the Association of Charities for co-operative work and directly led thereto, the same men being active leaders in each agitation. In other instances, as in Philadelphia, city outdoor relief was abandoned because the Charity Organization Societies stood ready to make it needless. It was a distribution of alms very much suspected as contribution to political corruption; and where its administration escaped this suspicion there was little responsibility for the individual application of the appropriation, and less investigation into the needs and habits of the recipients. The mere existence of an appropriation from the public treasury was demoralizing to the poor, who thought they had a right to a share in it and felt no gratitude for so impersonal and official a dole. It would be gratifying, if the statistics were to be had, to show what Charity Organization has done directly in lightening the tax-payers' burden; but this is a matter of minor significance compared with the more humane remedial aims of the movement. Only eight societies have supplied definite figures, and the results are given in this table : —

Brooklyn,— abolished in 1878 ; amount appropriated in 1877, ... $141,207.00
Buffalo,— average reduction, 50 per cent.; amount saved per annum, . 50,000.00
Burlington, Ia.,— reduction in one year, ... 4,000.00
Hartford, Conn.,— reduction, 65 per cent.; amount saved per annum, . 26,000.00
Indianapolis,— reduction, 91 per cent.; amount appropriated in 1880
   less than in 1876 (this city now reports applications for aid re-
   duced one-half), ... 82,000.00
New Haven, Conn.,— reduction in one year (also one relief society's
   expenditure fell from $2,000 to $500), ... 10,000.00
Omaha, Neb.,— reduction in one year, ... 15,000.00
Philadelphia,— abolished in 1880; average appropriations to
   1879, ... $66,000
   Less outdoor medical relief continued, averaging per year
   about 6,000   60,000.00
Syracuse,— reduction, 43 per cent.; amount saved per annum, . . . 10,850.00
Taunton, Mass.,— abolished, ... 10,423.00

Total present annual reduction, ... $409,480.00

Besides this sum, in Cincinnati and Minneapolis the municipal outdoor relief has diminished one-half, notwithstanding the increase of population. Albany and Portland, Ore., note its decrease. In Detroit its distribution has been turned over to a special commission appointed by the mayor and presumably removed from partisan political control. In Newark it has been restricted to bread and coal tickets during the three winter months, but is continued to widows and the aged the year round. In Lawrence and Malden, Mass., Newburg, N.Y., Plainfield, N.J., San Francisco, Springfield, Ohio, and Waterbury, Conn., it has been administered with increasing discrimination, while from Boston it is reported that the Overseers of the Poor make more thorough investigation, more rigidly exclude persons able to support themselves and those addicted to drink or vice.

Street Begging.— From the important cities of Albany, Boston, Charleston, S.C., Cleveland, Davenport, Detroit, Newark, N.J., New Haven, Omaha, Philadelphia, Portland, Ore., Rochester, N.Y., San Francisco, Syracuse, and Waterbury, Conn., information comes that street begging has been perceptibly diminished. In five of these cities it is pronounced suppressed, which means at least the mendicants no longer flaunt their rags and deformities before the eyes of citizens or wail their dolorous cant in the public ear. Albany and Davenport send the touching words that child-begging has ceased. New York deals energetically with this imposture, employing two special officers to deal with this class of cases. An analyzed record is kept of the cases; and in 1892 63.4 per cent. were found to be inmates of cheap lodging-houses and police stations, 20.7 to have homes, and 2.9 could not be traced to any abode. Of these 79 per cent. were able-bodied, and 21 per cent. were maimed, sick, or aged. To give to these maimed and aged ones on the streets was cruelty, as it kept them from the more humane and adequate provision of the almshouse. Instructed in all cases to offer the services of the society for the relief of apparent necessity, the officers caused the arrest and imprisonment of 48 per cent., warned 44 per cent. to desist from begging, and the rest were either put beyond the society's reach by the magistrate or referred to the care of some church or district committee. These are the only records within reach that permit a study and classification of the street-beggar genus, and probably the ratios here given will hold good for the whole class throughout the country. This work in New York, Boston, and Buffalo is impeded by the custom there of granting licenses to maimed and afflicted persons to play musical instruments and to peddle small wares on the street, under which guise much soliciting of alms from passers-by takes place.

Vagrants.— The homeless and the wanderers furnish a class known in poor-law legislation as vagrants. Whether these be sturdy vagabonds or dislodged unfortunates, Charity Organization aims to end their vagrancy by placing them again in some sort of social relations, either by force of law or by some sifting process which separates the curable from the chronic cases. In the repression of vagrancy three resources have been employed,— the police for the incorrigible and dissolute, labor tests as a means of discriminating those who have abandoned themselves to a predatory career from those who are willing to use the means afforded for reaching self-support, and lodgings where wayfarers may abide temporarily while in pursuit of employment. Some of the Wayfarers' Lodges employ labor tests, but the favorite form of such tests is the wood-yard. The oldest and most systematic of these combined lodges and tests is in Boston, where the city took up the work in 1879. It at once relieved the police station houses of the "casuals," and spared the unfortunates who were desirous of self-maintenance the humiliation and contamination of police stations. Here, too, the purification of the person and the clothing of the beneficiaries were scrupulously attended to, accompanied by the strong re-enforcement of that cleanliness which restores one's self-respect. This system has also been carried to a wide extent in Philadelphia ; and here the Charity Organization Society, at its own expense, performs for the city the work of relieving the station houses and streets from the casuals. Upon this department the society spent 54 per cent. in 1892 of the income of its Central Treasury (or $14,911.33), and was reimbursed by sales from the wood-yard to the extent of 66 per cent. ($9,984.59), and by an appropriation from the State of 23.4 per cent. ($3,500 a year). This system is regarded there as the most successful and beneficent department of the general work of the society. It comprises two separate agencies, one for dealing with non-residents, of whom half are received from the City Department of Public Safety. Every effort is made to return these casuals to their kindred or the towns where they had domiciles, and facilities for doing this are freely granted by the transportation companies. The labor tests are chiefly connected with the Wayfarers' Lodges, where 15,476 wanderers found shelter and assistance in 1892. The work of the society in the rural district of Bryn Mawr is chiefly of this kind. It may be said that the encouragement of labor tests is a prevalent purpose of Charity Organization Societies everywhere, whether controlled by them or set up by municipal authority or by other societies. The system, being necessarily compulsory to a large extent, requires the co-operation of the police authorities, which is usually easily obtained, since it releases them from the care of thousands who are charged with no misdemeanor, and who ought not to be taken before a magistrate. It is reported to us that twenty-seven of our societies in dealing with this vagabondage lodged 70.9 per cent. and subjected 26 per cent. to labor tests. This distinction between lodging and labor tests does not, however. seem trustworthy, since, as a rule, both are practised in combination.

In addition, 117 cases of fraudulent schemes, especially those pretending to be organizations for charitable purposes, were detected and exposed, and in some cases broken up, in 1892, by far the greater part of this suppression having occurred in New York City.

Co-operation.- The very name of Charity Organization indicates a paramount purpose to bring about the co-operation of those engaged in ministering to the poor and unfortunate. In so far as this result remains unattained, the practice of Charity Organization falls below its theory and standards. The scheme of registration was devised to compass this end, investigation is meant to facilitate it, the restriction upon Friendly Visitors in the matter of almsgiving is based upon it. Yet co-operation is one of the most difficult of attainments. Various causes obstruct the work of our societies in this direction. In some cities there exists a distinct hostility in the older charitable societies to Charity Organization. They resent the implication that their work may need amending or they are unwilling to submit to any outside judgment. But more common by far is the simple inertia of churches and societies. They do not oppose : they often approve our principles and aims ; but they do not take the trouble to keep records, report cases, or consult the registration bureaus. Co-operation is a thing of slow growth, but each advance made and held is a distinct and decisive triumph of organization ideals. Out of forty societies embraced in this branch of our inquiry, thirty-one claim a co-operation, more or less complete, with municipal agencies of relief. The ratio thereof is the high one of 97 per cent., and it is gratifying to learn that in some important centres it is cordial and unrestrained. The returns of thirty societies show that together they have established a practical co-operation with one-third of the charitable agencies and institutions in their cities. Our inquiries have elicited the unexpected and gratifying fact that in thirty-four cities co-operation has been attained with 44 per cent. of the churches located in them. So variously has the inquiry concerning co-operation with individuals been understood and answered that no useful generalization can be made about it. It was intended to elicit the number of persons immediately engaged in some work of compassion for a family or an individual, who had used the records or investigations or agencies of Charity Organization in effecting their purpose. The matter is obscure, and must be passed here without further remark than that the reports from the larger towns and cities are quite uniformly encouraging.

Registration.— It is a singular mark of the general and deep impression upon the public mind concerning the imposture and worthlessness of applications for relief that registration and investigation should be regarded as a sort of detective and repressive system. This feature of Charity Organization is to the popular and superficial mind the most obnoxious one of our work. Yet the dread that light thrown upon pauperism would reveal the great extent of its mendacity and vicious origin is in truth a most forcible argument against indiscriminate, dissociated, and disorderly almsgiving. It is true that registration and investigation form a sieve that separates, with a practical justice, cases entitled by misfortune to material relief from those who would pervert such aid to the prolongation of self-ruinous habits; but even then it does not remove from humane care those who are technically called "undeserving." It only creates a classification which dictates different modes of treatment. It is essential that the physician should know what ails his patient before he prescribes, and not give a splint to the consumptive and cod-liver oil to the man with broken bones. The good Samaritan knew better than to set the robber on his ass, or to give the wounded wayfarer only his pence, or expend his wine and oil on the able-bodied landlord.

But the detective and repressive effects of registration and investigation are but incidental to them under present social conditions. Their true purpose is far greater and grander, and were all imposture and dishonest design to cease in the field of pauperism there would still be need of these two processes. The information accumulated by them not only lays bare the false address, the professional beggar, and the slum-degraded debauchee, but, on the other hand, it maintains the cause of the upright poor, and supplies their credentials to sympathy and help. It would not abolish overlapping, but adjust it so that the alms from one source may complement the alms from another, and so concert them that they may be timely, appropriate, and adequate. But, above all, it is the key to co-operation. The records of the registration bureau enable the Charity Organizationist to say to all who toil for the relief of penury: "We have that information which is invaluable to you, if you would do your work wisely and efficiently. We cannot compel co-operation, but we can serve you, and by service become your auxiliary and friend."

There are two sides to registration. Societies and individuals may make use of our archives for guidance in administering their own relief, and they may also enlarge our records by reporting the families and persons whom they aid. The first form of co-operation is by far the more common: it is much rarer for churches, societies, and private almsgivers to report to us their own operations. Often this default is not from lack of approval of our aims and work, nor from want of cordial sympathy and intercourse, but simply owing to the need of adopting unwonted methods and the labor required in the systematic exchange of information. Were our bureaus of registration replenished and used as the Charity Organization theory requires, the active benevolences of society would fall into alignment, and move as a disciplined army, animated with a common purpose, each company supporting the others, to the conquest of the problems of penury, misery, and degradation. It seems incredible that the nine-tenths of society which is whole and sound cannot in due time concert measures, and unitedly work them out, which would renovate the other tenth.

Administrators of public official relief recognize that they are the servants of society, and responsible to it for the way in which they perform their work; and hence they are the most willing to open their records to our societies. In New England, however, outside of Boston and Newport, the Overseers of the Poor seem reticent and obstructive. In eleven * large cities it is claimed that the bureaus of registration are working in unrestricted harmony and completeness with poor-law officials. Minneapolis and New Haven estimate that their records cover nine-tenths of the municipal relief cases: in Albany, Buffalo, and Rochester the ratio ranges from one to three-quarters; and in three other cities this form of co-operation is returned as partial or considerable. Registration for other voluntary societies is returned for only twelve cities, and ranges from 25 per cent. of such societies in Lynn, Mass., to 90 per cent. in New York and New Haven. Doubtless, as in New York, many of these societies register only the cases on which they desire to consult the central records. In Boston 35 per cent. of the cases taken

* They are Boston, Burlington, Ia., Cincinnati, Detroit, Milwaukee, Newark, N.J., Newport, R.I., New York, Salem, Mass., Seattle, Wash., and Syracuse.

up by the Associated Charities are referred thither by other charitable societies. The average extent of this exchange would appear to be with 59 per cent. of the recognized voluntary charities of twelve cities. Fourteen societies have registered for churches, reporting from 10 to 80 per cent. of the whole number in their communities to be pledged to the principle, but registering (as in the case of societies) with varying degrees of fidelity. New York taking the lead. Such service for asylums and similar private institutions is naturally restricted, as their beneficiaries are less fluctuating in numbers, and admission to them is of a more formal character. For eight societies the registration service has extended to from five to seventy-five per cent. of the whole number of such institutions, New Haven leading. In some societies registration has been found cumbersome, and is not systematically undertaken. In others, notably in Boston and New York, it is carried to constantly increasing efficiency, both as to fulness and accuracy of statistics and as to promptness in making the service available to others. As might be expected, the New York accumulated records are very large, and embrace at least 170,000 families or parts of families. Where this work has been well maintained, our societies find it invaluable, as well for their own visitors as for promoting co-operation, and commending their work to other societies and to philanthropic minds.

In 1886 a plan was proposed in Buffalo of a central registration bureau for all the Charity Organization Societies, which should confine itself to recording, travelling, and professional mendicants. It was a scheme for the suppression of "rounders," or professional, genteel, travelling mendicants, but proved to be premature; for there were not enough registering societies to make it effective.

SOCIAL STATE.— Another important plan was devised at the same time for the classification of applicants for relief according to their family relations, ages, and nationality. It is mentioned in this connection because it involves the methods and details of registration. It went into fairly general operation in 1889, when the blank forms were agreed upon and published by action of this National Conference. (See Appendix II.) It is based on the joint experience of the American societies, and elicited the approval of the first International Conference of Charities held in Paris,— a Conference, by the way, which declared the Charity Organization Societies of Great Britain and the United States to be the most wisely contrived and efficient agencies for dealing with the social problems of penury and misfortune known to it. It is highly gratifying to state that the gathering of materials for this report elicited the fact that thirty-one of our most important Organization Societies have, with commendable completeness, adhered to the plan, and kept valuable records. A brief summary of the results reached may be given as follows. Of over 15,000 cases reported,

34.59 per cent. were married couples.
19.03 " " " widows.
6.55 " " " deserted wives.
6.30 " " " single women.
3.74 " " " widowers or deserted husbands.
25.84 " " " single men.
1.09 " " " orphaned or abandoned children.

Of over 35,000 cases reported,—

46.52 per cent. were under 20 years of age (four-fifths of these were mere children).
9.65 per cent. were between 20 and 40 years.
32.42 " " " " 40 and 55 years.
19.40 " " " " 55 and 70 years.
Only 1.66 " " " over 70.

Of 21,700 cases reported,—

42.21 per cent. were white persons born in the United States.
8.58 " " " colored persons born in the United States.
3.52 " " " Canadians.
5.60 " " " British.
11.94 " " " German.
19.54 " " " Irish.
1.53 " " " Scandinavians.
1.77 " " " Poles and Russians.

The rest were of miscellaneous origin in very small ratios. Of over 6,600 cases,—

75.77 per cent. could both read and write.
5.84 " " " read, but not write.
18.39 " " " neither read nor write.

If it were in the province of this report to forsake the ground of simple retrospection and history, it would be interesting to comment on these social conditions; but the studious philanthropist will find in the tables accompanying the report material for his own instructive generalizations. Yet a word may be said here to enforce the value of keeping uniform records, so that ample and trustworthy statistics may be had. Charity Organization is far from claiming that the problems of pauperism have been solved. It only promises that they shall be studied, so that the causes and sources of misery may be discovered and appropriate methods for dealing with its manifold forms adopted. Our societies are the only agencies in the United States through which authentic statistics can be gathered, not only covering a census of relief-seekers, but eliciting the causes of pauperism and exhibiting the results of various methods of dealing with it. This sort of information, if carefully collected and collated, will soon become a treasury of details to which the sociologist will confidently resort, and on which legislators, reformers, and workers among the poor have already begun to base their courses of conduct. The function is one of wide public importance, and is well worth performing.

Sanitary Work.— Improvement of the hygienic conditions of humble life comes to Charity Organization Societies only as an incident of dealing with special, and these generally desperate, cases of bad domiciles. It is a matter ultimately controlled by legislation, and this depends on the diffusion of information as to the necessity for and the modes of doing it. The subject will be returned to later on ; but our societies in the larger cities have given it much painstaking consideration, and seldom lose it from sight. The methods used by them are appeals to landlords and to boards of health in particular cases, the removal of their beneficiaries from unwholesome quarters, the promotion of open-air excursions for women and children, and the obtaining of country homes for those who will remove to them. (See Appendix G.)

CLASSIFIED DISPOSITION OF CASES. (See Appendix I.) — From the beginning Charity Organization Societies in the United States have followed a plan of recording the disposition made of applicants whose cases came under their charge, which conformed in a general way to that of the great parent society in London. Modifications of it necessarily have taken place to suit the conditions of each locality, and it is probable that in minor phases of the work no two societies are alike. But the general outlines are preserved, and to the tabulation of such statistics a larger number of societies have contributed than to any other department of this report. There are forty-four of them whose reports have been received, and these embrace the treatment given to the huge number of nearly 75,000 cases. With the exception of a few cities, this number embraces only new and not recurrent applications, and hence represents the fresh expansion of the work in the year 1892. Of this total, 4.76 per cent. were adjudged to require continuous relief because of orphanage, age, or chronic disability; 24.84 per cent. needed the temporary aid which combats an emergency, as of sickness or injury or the cessation of wages; employment would have released 16.05 per cent. from the necessity of asking any alms, were they disposed to labor honestly to get their own living; 3.39 per cent. had means of their own or relatives able to provide for them; 10.33 per cent. were of such profligate habits that any merchandisable relief would have prolonged their dissolute self-indulgence; 1.58 per cent. were placed in institutions; 7.72 per cent. were put in charge of religious organizations or of voluntary charitable societies; for only 0.76 per cent. was the interference of the police authorities invoked; for but 0.89 per cent. was recourse had to municipal relief officers, to supplement the care of private charity; for 11.13 per cent. churches, synagogues, and humane societies wrought in co-operation with our societies; for 6.6 per cent. individual citizens supplied all or a part of the aid required; 0.8 per cent. were enabled by loans to establish themselves in some form of industry; for 18.04 per cent. was employment obtained; 0.65 per cent. were removed to new situations or the care of kindred. The efforts of sixteen societies are estimated to have brought to self-maintenance 1,524 cases, or 2.04 per cent.; but this item is far below the facts, inasmuch as many of the larger societies have, for various reasons, discontinued computing and recording these recoveries to independence. Owing to the different methods of keeping their records, and of making the returns compiled in the reports of the various societies, exact deductions cannot be made, and the same cases must appear in two or more classes. In some returns only new applicants are recorded. In others, as in Brooklyn and Philadelphia, recurrent cases are included. But recurrent cases also form part of the year's work. It is probable, therefore, that a tide of over 100,000 families and individuals flowed through the conduits of the Charity Organization Societies. If they are grouped in large generalizations, those who need employment being placed, as for the most part shirkers of labor, with the vicious and those having resources sufficient to make beggary unjustifiable, and those receiving loans counted with those assisted to labor, it may be affirmed as approximately true that three-tenths of this vast array of alms-seekers really need material succor, and an equal number do not need it at all; of the charge of one-tenth our societies have been wholly relieved by placing them in other care, which has been freely and cordially supplied; for nearly one-fifth the co-operation of other societies and of individuals and municipal officers has been obtained; and for one-fifth relief by employment was found adequate. It is probable that these ratios fairly represent the experience thus far of those engaged in Charity Organization work and methods.

PROVIDENT SCHEMES. (See Appendix H.) - Graduation from dependence to self-maintenance is an expression which, if it did not originate among the Charity Organizationists of Boston, is at least familiar to all engaged in this work throughout the United States. It describes the aim of the reforms of relief systems, and the degree of achievement in it is the supreme test of our principles. If there is to be no elevation of our wards into self-support, then Charity Organization Societies only add to the alms-doling of which the consequences have been so pernicious to society. Whatever may educate the downcast to the standards, habits, and sentiments essential to self-maintenance, and free them from the need of the intervention of others, commands the hearty advocacy and re-enforcement of our societies. Far beyond the provident schemes which they control has been the influence they have exerted in inducing others to promote and support enterprises for the propagation of thrift, frugality, skill in the common affairs of life, and an honorable self-respect. Thus in cities where Charity Organization Societies have been planted and acquired their characteristic influence there has been a very conspicuous contemporaneous growth in the number and variety of provident enterprises. And our societies claim that this is not a mere chance, but the direct result of their teachings, and generally the result of the personal labors of their own members. For example, the kindergarten system of the public schools of Philadelphia began with an association formed among the ladies of the Charity Organization Society, and they ceased not to labor until their work was taken up by the Board of Education during the superintendency of Dr. McAllister; and the present grand development of industrial education and manual training in that city was inaugurated and nursed by the same society. The Associated Charities of Boston directly controls few provident schemes; but persons active in the direction of that association have promoted co-operative savings-banks and building associations and seen the day nurseries double in ten years, kindergartens become a part of the public school system, and industrial schools double. In Brooklyn the founder of the Pratt Institute was an earlier counsellor and advocate of the Bureau of Charities. In New York day nurseries have multiplied eightfold, kindergartens nearly as rapidly, boys' clubs, working-girls' associations, and manual training schools have been opened, and savings funds have been started. Remarkable expansion of like agencies is reported from Cincinnati, Detroit, and other important cities. Buffalo took the lead in establishing crèches, or nurseries where mothers could leave their infants to be cared for while they went to their day's work; and now there are twenty-two cities in which one hundred and five such institutions have been established at the instigation or under the control of Organization Societies. As many cities maintain over one hundred and forty-eight kindergartens. Laundries, work-rooms, cooking, sewing, and other industrial schools have in like manner been called into existence.

Savings Funds.—In seventeen cities Charity Organization Societies control penny savings funds. These are of four sorts : simple Provident Societies, taking small deposits at the counter : Stamp Banks, where deposit stamps are sold at stations in different parts of the city,— Boston having one hundred and twenty-three, and New York two hundred and six stations ; and Funds to receive small deposits gathered by visitors, who call at houses for them, as in Newport, R.I., and Castleton, S.I.,— an ingenious system, which combines with great effectiveness the work of the Friendly Visitor with the encouragement of savings ; and Fuel Funds, by means of which the deposits of the summer secure deliveries of wood and coal in the winter at cost price. Eighteen such provident fund organizations were known to exist in 1892 under the auspices of our societies, gathering in the savings of 33,826 depositors. The habits of self-restraint and thrift thus inculcated among the very poor are invaluable, and among the best of defences against the spread of pauperism among the depositors. (See Appendix H.)

Distribution by States.- Of the Charity Organization Societies, and those in correspondence with them with adjustments to their principles, existing in 1892, there are sixteen in the State of New York. fourteen in Massachusetts, eight in New Jersey, five in Ohio, four in Connecticut, three each in Maine, Rhode Island, Pennsylvania, Colorado, Indiana, Wisconsin, California, two each in Iowa, Michigan, Illinois, Kentucky, Nebraska, Minnesota, Missouri, and one each in South Carolina, Tennessee, Louisiana, Oregon, Delaware, and Washington State. In other words, the movement has established itself in twenty-nine cities of the Middle Atlantic States north of the Potomac, in twenty-four cities of New England, in eleven cities of States north of the Ohio, in eleven cities between the Mississippi and the Rocky Mountains, in seven cities in the old South, and in five cities of the Pacific States. There are eighteen States in which it has not penetrated. It has had its most rapid extension in the cities of the North Atlantic seaboard and of the Pacific Coast. In agricultural States the development has been slow: for evident reasons its expansion has an affinity with commerce. Also, it may be observed that the movement has thus far had but little development in towns predominantly manufacturing or interested in mining, and hence the interesting question arises as to how far trades-unions, labor federations, and the mutual benefit societies, so common and so influential among artisans and mechanics, render the services of Charity Organization superfluous.

SPECIAL LINES OF DEVELOPMENT. *Attitude toward Relief.—* As each community has its distinctive characteristics, so each Charity Organization Society inevitably adjusts itself to them, and diversities of practice and development spring up. These variations are desirable as enlarging the number of experiments tried and as throwing side-lights upon special problems. In one particular there is a growing unison of judgment. In the returns of the sixty societies contributing to this report there is no advocacy or defence of relief-giving from their own treasuries. On the contrary, those societies which practise it either deprecate or excuse it. In some instances, it is justified as a necessity growing out of the lack of other charitable agencies; in others, as a means of forcing on a retrenchment of municipal out-relief, especially where overseers of the poor refuse information and co-operation; in still others, it is explained as grounded in the fact

that the community does not understand or kindly receive our principles, and will not sustain a society that is purely administrative.
Again, it is apologized for as the effectual means of bringing all the
benevolent work of a community into one system and control. In
several cities the societies affirm that they are receding from the
distribution of alms, and desire to abandon it. All this testimony is
a distinct indication of the advance of our principles, and of an intelligent perception of the function of Charity Organization. The
matter is of prime importance, for upon this rock of almsgiving many
a society has been wrecked. It was nine years from the formation
of the London Society to the foundation of the first Charity
Organization Society in this country. Its literature and arguments
were republished here, nor was a knowledge of Chalmers's work in
Glasgow and of the reform movements in Hamburg, Leipzig and
Elberfeld unknown. Associations for Improving the Condition of
the Poor were formed under this and other names in several American cities, and they avowed principles which Charity Organization
could only reiterate; but they lapsed into mere dispensers of physical aid. In the history of the movement derived from London there
are wrecks along the way. Some of our societies have withdrawn
from the field, and others have degenerated from like causes. There
is in benevolent work a constant tendency to degenerate into mere
almsgiving,— a fact easily explained, for relief of this sort is easily
accomplished, the statistics of results are more imposing, and the
value of moral, educational, and personal forces in mitigating social
evils the public mind has not learned to estimate aright.   •

The existence in a city of an association professedly devoted to
the welfare of the poor, but which expressly announces that it
gathers no funds for supplying material relief, is a phenomenon cer-
tain to attract attention. Men will ask: "What does it do? What
are the reasons of its being?" In this way it begins to exert an
influence on the administration of other funds and other societies
and upon individuals. From dispassionate and careful observers it
is learned that in many cities official outdoor relief, where not abolished, has become more discriminating, that the management of
voluntary charities has become more circumspect and elevating, and
that personal almsgiving has been accompanied with a clearer sense
of responsibility. In two conspicuous instances — Lawrence, Mass.,
and Cleveland, Ohio,— there was a fairly complete readjustment on

the part of the leading general relief societies of each city to Charity Organization principles.

Adaptations.— In adapting themselves to the conditions existing in different communities, our societies have found a law of development which gives to each especial characteristics. Thus the co-operation of the police in Buffalo was the beginning there of the registration system, and gave the society a close relation to municipal relief; while the munificent Fitch trusts gave a vigorous impulse to the elaboration of provident and hospital schemes. Bridgeport, Conn., has directed its efforts especially toward women and children, providing instruction in sewing, kitchen-garden work, day nurseries, and a labor bureau. Lynn engages in all-around work, its one woman registrar doing the duty of a society for the prevention of cruelty to children and of a children's aid society. Boston, besides its own conferences on treatment of cases, has maintained a conference of representative delegates from the charitable societies and institutions of the city, where problems of general humane interest are discussed and modes of alleviating various forms of suffering are formulated. Philadelphia, after experimenting with many educational, labor, and provident schemes, made dealing with the homeless and wayfaring the characteristic work of its central office, in which Bryn Mawr, a place exposed to the tramp nuisance, followed. Indianapolis established a Loan Association, a Friendly Inn, and a Board of Children's Guardians which commanded especial interest. Salem, Mass., found gratification in supplying baby-carriages to poor families. Several of our principal societies emphasize registration and investigation, and have brought their bureaus to a highly orderly system and a prompt effectiveness. One large society (Philadelphia) claims that relief has become much more prompt of application,— a claim in direct contravention to the popular belief that investigation retards assistance. The favorite and more general relief expedient is found in employment offices and labor tests, and the most widely and deeply felt hindrance to effective work is reported to be the insufficiency of trained and persistent Friendly Visitors.

Friendly Visiting.— An ideal which most of the strongly organized societies have sought to attain, with varying degrees of success, has been that of inducing men and women having strength of character to go to the homes of the needy, each taking the chief responsibility for the proper development, material and moral, of a few families.

The societies in Boston, Brooklyn, Baltimore, and Cincinnati, have been most successful in carrying out this plan, and commend its usefulness with enthusiasm. Other societies, however, report that their effort to find visitors of sufficient judgment and experience to undertake the delicate and responsible work of properly helping a family has had meagre results.

Causes for this lack of success may be found, first, in the great burden entailed by proper registration and by examination of conditions in our largest cities, which leave comparatively little free energy for securing and training visitors. A second cause is found in the great pressure of life upon well-to-do people in large cities, leaving little time for personal service in the distant homes of the poor. A third lies in the comparative ignorance on the part of cultivated people of "how the other half lives." This ignorance, of course, disqualifies. Not until the churches awake with enthusiasm to caring for our less fortunate neighbors in the wise and helpful good Samaritan spirit will there be sufficient attention brought to bear upon the mass of poverty to have appreciable effect. The forces at command are too limited. It may be said, however, that where the Charity Organization Society has taken hold of the work of friendly visiting in earnest, as in Boston, the experience of the visitors has had its effect in developing higher standards of duty in church life.

Emergencies.— A peculiar and severe test of Charity Organization Societies has come in the demands made by special emergencies. The Chicago Relief and Aid Society reached a position of commanding influence, and was led to the adoption of many of these principles by acting as the distributor of the large funds contributed for the aid of sufferers by the great fire of 1872. All agencies familiar with the poor and with relief came into immediate co-operation. Under this system the work was rapidly carried on, and the Relief and Aid Society established relations so friendly and intimate with other charitable organizations that it has been able ever since to maintain a commanding position in the confidence of the people of that city.

Boston was moved to the steps which resulted in her Associated Charities by the suffering consequent upon its great fire of 1872, and on the commercial crisis which began in 1873 and brooded over the land for two or three years. The Malden (Mass.) society was formed to alleviate the distress caused by a great fire in 1875.

When the disastrous flood of February, 1884, prevailed at Cincinnati, by which five hundred and four families were driven from their homes and otherwise involved in such distress as compelled them to appeal for help, recourse was had at once to the services of the Associated Charities. The official report states that that society "entered most heartily into the work, and through their thoroughly organized district societies distributed large quantities of supplies throughout the flooded sections of the city with great discretion and without waste." The authorities publicly acknowledged the debt of gratitude owing to the members of the Associated Charities " who so zealously devoted their time and thoughtful labor to the assistance of the committee in its charitable work." The labor undertaken by the Associated Charities may be estimated from the fact that $194,-400 was contributed to relieve the misery caused by the flood, of which $91,400 was locally distributed : and upon that society depended largely the discreet distribution of relief, and the protection of the funds from the assaults of imposture.

At the time of the terrible Johnstown flood the District of Columbia Committee to gather aid for the sufferers sent the secretary of the Associated Charities of Washington thither as their agent. His experience was of immediate value in not only bringing the relief work into order, but in providing methods by which sturdy and clamorous petitioners for help were repressed, women, aged and feeble persons obtained due and equal consideration, and the early miscarriages of relief were effectively corrected. The agent found occasion to lament that Johnstown did not afford that information concerning its poor inhabitants and that supply of competent workers which Charity Organization acquires where it has been established.

In 1889 a disastrous fire swept over an area of twenty-five acres in Lynn, rendering one hundred and seventy-five families homeless, and putting seven thousand persons out of employment. The information accumulated by the Associated Charities, covering many families, was instantly available. The skill of its visitors, agents, and managers, came into immediate requisition for the preparation of record blanks and the systematizing of the distribution of food, clothing, and shelter. A delegation of experienced visitors came from the society in Boston, and during the six days in which a more general relief committee was taking form and acquiring funds and stores the Associated Charities was giving order and shaping meth ods which alleviated immediate distress and facilitated subsequent operations. Then the registration, personal knowledge, and experience due to Charity Organization proved to be invaluable for promptness and efficacy.

The tornado of Louisville in May, 1890, by which seventy-six lives were lost and two hundred persons were injured, created great suffering. The Board of Trade Relief Committee expended $156,000 in alleviating it, and employed the visitors and agents of the Charity Organization Society as its investigators and almoners. Their knowledge and expertness were indispensable. When in the same year Lawrence (Mass.) was swept by a cyclone by which eight persons were killed, twenty-one severely injured, and many buildings were damaged or destroyed, the city authorities called upon our local society to plan, organize and administer the needed relief. In the Park Place disaster in New York, May, 1891, when sixty-three persons were killed or injured, those in charge of the Mayor's Relief Fund invoked the aid of the Charity Organization Society, and within a week the particulars of each case were collected, and recommendations made which were followed in the distribution of the fund contributed for the sufferers. By the same means the $7,000 collected by the New York *Herald* for the same disaster were disbursed. Acknowledgment was made by the Mayor's Committee in these terms : "We realize that only experienced and skilful agents could make so satisfactory reports within so short a time, and congratulate the city that it has a society which can render such efficient aid in times of sudden emergency." This capacity to act in emergencies cannot seem strange to those who consider the readiness for prompt work secured by a registration bureau, by a large staff of trained agents and visitors familiar with the aspects of want, and by a co-operative scheme which embraces the whole field of benevolent work among the destitute.

INDIRECT EFFECTS OF CHARITY ORGANIZATION.— It is to be observed that from its first appearance in America Charity Organization has surveyed the field in which it established itself, to discover what was lacking there and to devise better methods for improving the condition of the poor. Not solicitous of aggrandizement, it has been content to stimulate the creation of new educational and provident measures under independent control, and to which its administration might be supplementary. Consequently, many agencies have sprung into existence at its instigation, the work of which cannot be recorded as part of its annals. The influence of Charity Organization on municipal relief, on the inception and management of other charities, and on public sentiment, has been already sufficiently indicated. It should, however, be added that in Philadelphia the Children's Aid Society had its initial impulse among the active workers of the Charity Organization Society. In Indianapolis the society crushed out the Vincennes Lottery and waged war with the wine-rooms. The Denver society procured the creation of a State Board of Charities.

Legislation.— Not the least of the labors undertaken in this movement are the efforts to amend legislation. In Massachusetts the separation of the pauper from the criminal class in public institutions has been accomplished. There and in New York strenuous efforts have proceeded from our societies to restrict the sale of alcoholic liquors ; the poor-relief laws have been amended. In the same States the statutes have defined tenement-houses so as to bring a larger number under official inspection, new requirements have been imposed by sanitary laws, and in Boston an alliance has been made with the Technological Institute to examine and secure complaints and reports on the violation of sanitary principles. In New York a law has been secured authorizing the city to open municipal lodging-houses, to relieve the station houses of wayfarers and secure their cleanliness, but the provisions of the statute are still held in abeyance. Another was enacted providing for small parks and open spaces for play-grounds by the demolition of some of the worst squares of tenements in the overcrowded sections of the city; and immigration has been made a subject of careful investigation, and recommendations prepared for submission to Congress. When the fear of the spread of cholera in the summer of 1892 created the necessity for rigorous sanitary precautions in this country, the Charity Organization Society of Buffalo, through its Committee on Sanitary Condition of the Homes of the Poor, offered the services of its agents to the Health Commissioner as Sanitary Inspectors of tenement-houses. He gladly accepted these services. These agents made a thorough inspection of some five hundred tenements in the city of Buffalo, and obtained and collated a large amount not only of sanitary, but of sociological information as well. The result proved, to the satisfaction of the Committee on the Sanitary Condition of the Homes of the Poor, that gross abuses existed in the tenements of the city, which were due, on the one hand, to the lax building-laws of the city and the absence of rigorous regulations to govern the owners of tenement-houses, and, on the other hand, to the tenants themselves. As a result, the committee began an agitation for the adoption of a complete set of ordinances governing the construction and management of tenement-houses. Into this movement it drew the Buffalo Builders' Exchange and the Buffalo Chapter of the American Society of Architects. A number of meetings were held jointly of the Health Commissioner, the Commissioner of Buildings, a medical and legal member of the Committee on Sanitary Condition of the Homes of the Poor, a representative of the Builders' Exchange, and a representative of the Society of Architects, which resulted in the presentation to the Common Council of the city, by the Health Commissioner, of probably one of the most complete codes of ordinances governing the subject that has ever been framed. A great deal of pressure, stimulated by the committee and exerted on the Common Council, finally secured the adoption of these ordinances. In several societies there is a department of legal advice, in which professional service is rendered gratuitously to prevent injustice or secure the poor in their rights.

Education.— It is gratifying to note that since Charity Organization Societies began to be formed for the study of social problems, and to accumulate information and statistics concerning them, seminaries or departments for the investigation of like sociological questions have been established at Harvard, Yale, Johns Hopkins, Cornell, Pennsylvania, Vanderbilt, Leland Stanford, and Chicago Universities, at the State Universities of Ohio, Michigan, and Nebraska, at Amherst and Bryn Mawr Colleges, and in connection with some of these institutions occasional or serial papers are published from time to time. This subject was brought up at the Omaha Conference of Charities and Correction in 1887, and the introduction of the study of Charity Organization into high schools, colleges, and universities recommended. Representatives of our societies have been called upon to lecture on these themes in several colleges and theological seminaries, especially in the prominent ones in or within easy reach of the leading cities, and also before audiences assembled in churches.

Literature.— A list of papers, essays, and books issued by the

Charity Organization Societies of America, and distributed by them, is appended to this report. (See Appendix L.) The literature concerning the social problems of poverty is very large, and could not be enumerated here if it were pertinent to a report so specialized in the history of a single movement as this. Attention should be called here to the *Monthly Register*, which began with the first year of the Philadelphia Society, and has been continued ever since in that city. It has been accepted as a sort of representative organ by many sister societies, and is the oldest periodical controlled by a Charity Organization Society in the United States. *Lend a Hand* is a monthly edited by Rev. Dr. E. E. Hale, published in Boston and devoted to philanthropic work. The *Charities Review* was begun in November, 1891, by the New York society, and aims at a thorough and scientific treatment of charitable principles, methods, and administration. Cincinnati produces the *Children's Home Monthly*.

This report has abstained from reflections and recommendations almost wholly. Its scope was restricted in the original instructions of this Conference to the History of Charity Organization in the United States. Already it has grown voluminous, but it is simply retrospective. Had it been possible to obtain returns from all the Charity Organization Societies of the country as ample and painstaking as those from Boston, the results would have a greatly increased value. Such material as could be obtained has been collated here, and perhaps the student of philanthropy will find in its text and tables matter not unworthy of reflection. It may yet, with all its imperfections, prove to be the basis of future comparative study. The results which it is enabled to present, and which are below rather than above the actual facts, show that Charity Organization has taken firm root in America, that its expansion has been very rapid, that it is purifying itself and rising to higher standards, that its educational force is potent, and that it is a harbinger of the day when the charities of men shall add to the benefactions of the purse those of their brains, their hearts, and their faith.

NECROLOGY.

Only the sad task remains of inscribing on these pages the names of those who once wrought with us, imparted to us their hope, their tenderness, and their wisdom, and who have gone to repose on that exhaustless divine charity which their loving spirits bravely tried, as the power was given them, to emulate. Some few of the many whose memory and example remain as benedictions to their associates must have a tribute here to meet the demands of our hearts. They were our pioneers and well known in our councils. An appended paper supplies the names of those reported to your committee at this time. (See Appendix M.) It is much regretted that the list is so imperfect.

Hodge.— With happy sagacity the Philadelphia Society called H. Lenox Hodge, M.D., to be its first president. Of honored lineage, of high professional eminence, of winning sweetness of disposition, he uttered judgments so wise and conciliatory that the divergent opinions of his associates melted into unison before them. His great influence was a tower of strength to the nascent society, and his name entrenched it in public confidence. He embodied that "sweetness and light" which Matthew Arnold thought to give the soul its noblest excellence. He died in the strength of his manhood and while president of the society.

McCulloch.— Rev. Oscar C. McCulloch was a magician of philanthropy. His was a scholar's diligence and enthusiasm in the study of the alleviation of human misery. No man was more dexterous in detecting the dictates of true charity and following them through the complexities and discords of social benevolence, for in his heart was the divine instinct which "beareth all things, believeth all things, hopeth all things." The Charity Organization Society of Indianapolis, founded under his leadership, is his monument ; and to future generations may it long transmit his honored fame.

Vanderpoel.— During the first three years of its history the Charity Organization Society of New York enjoyed the leadership of Dr. S. O. Vanderpoel, when failing health compelled him to relinquish his presidency, and soon after (March 12, 1886) he died. His mature judgment, varied experience, conscientious diligence, and unvarying courtesy were invaluable to the society.

Johnston.— In September of the year 1886 Colles Johnston died, an earnest and faithful worker upon a district committee, and much in direct contact with the poor. Mr. Johnston brought to the service of the society an unusual degree of intelligent devotion, of wise discrimination, of fidelity to his assumed duties, and of strength and sweetness of character.

Minturn.— Robert B. Minturn, vice-president of the New York society and one of its original promoters, followed his colleague to the grave in 1891. His character secured public confidence, his counsels strengthened the society, his purse generously contributed to its support.

DuBois.— Mrs. Cornelius DuBois, one of the leading philanthropic spirits of this generation, died in 1888, a strenuous friend and upholder of the New York society in her official relations with other local institutions.

Tuckerman.— Lucius Tuckerman was an original active member of the council, of great wisdom and experience, and during his life a liberal supporter of the Society. He died in 1890.

Gibbons.— The New York society endured bereavement last year in the death of Mrs. Abby Hopper Gibbons. She was the daughter of Isaac T. Hopper, renowned in his day for his anti-slavery activity. Reaching the unusual age of ninety-two, her last venerable years were employed in leading the societies she still actively managed and counselled into co-operation in Charity Organization. Weight of years served to ripen her undaunted energy and far-seeing wisdom.

Preston.— Vicar-General Thomas S. Preston, who died last year, was an earnest and useful friend of the society in New York, and an efficient intermediary in all negotiations with the authorities and agencies of the Roman Catholic Church.

Brooks.— " By the death of Phillips Brooks the Associated Charities of Boston lost one of its most beloved and inspiring friends. He was on the first committee appointed to report a plan of organization and co-operation, and on the provisional council until the society was organized." It is recorded that " his eloquence and his great influence have been repeatedly exerted in the society's behalf. His ability and still more his personal character were such that whatever he touched gained from him beauty and dignity. His eloquent words at the various public meetings of the society set forth the scope of its work and the spirit that should pervade it in a way that exalted and ennobled it for all who heard him."

The Boston society also laments the loss of Mrs. James Lodge and Miss Mary Anne Wales, and a co-worker thus records the sense of bereavement : —

Wales.— " Miss Wales was distinguished by her untiring devotion to her work long after disease had laid its hand upon her. Her chief happiness and the occupation of her life was in spending her money and herself in deeds of benevolence."

Lodge.— " Mrs. Lodge's gayety of heart, the pleasure she took in doing kindnesses, made her a constant source of cheerfulness and encouragement to her fellow-workers. To her and to Mrs. James T. Fields the society owes the first experiment in organized friendly visiting, which was the beginning of its success."

Pratt. Charles Pratt, whose desire to elevate the depressed by bringing to them skill and discipline in industrial arts led him to found the munificent Pratt Institute of Brooklyn, was one of the founders and liberal upholders of the Bureau of Charities in that city.

Buzelle.— Of George B. Buzelle, the general secretary of the Brooklyn society from its inception until his death, it was declared, as his body was laid to rest: " He was one of God's noblemen. He had caught the spirit of his Master's words: 'Whosoever will be great among you shall be your minister. Whosoever of you shall. be chiefest shall be servant of all.' He was not a hireling, he was not an official, - he was a man and a brother. No one could have known Mr. Buzelle without being impressed with his faithfulness. Nothing could stand between him and his duty." The chairman of this committee as his nearest neighbor in like responsibility, and all who have known him in these Conferences, and especially in the painstaking and eminently successful labors of this chairmanship a year ago, will testify that these words cover no exaggerations.

Osborn.— The first person to contribute to the Organized Charities Association of New Haven, Mrs. Walter Osborn, continued its generous friend until her death last year. She was a conspicuous supporter of all enterprises of the university city designed to make the lives of the lowly and indigent ampler and better.

Dunlap.—Mrs. Harriet A. Dunlap, was one of the most devoted, intelligent, and efficient women of Syracuse, and was president of several of its largest and oldest charitable institutions. A faithful friend, worker, and officer of the Bureau of Labor and Charities. She died in 1884.

Minor.— In the same city Rev. Ovid Minor, a Congregational minister, died in 1891. He was especially devoted to the care and rescue of children from neglect and exposure. A warm philanthropist, he was an indefatigable worker for the improvement of society.

Judson. — The Syracuse Bureau of Labor and Charities also recalls the cordial friendship and diligence of Mrs. Sarah Judson, a gentlewoman of invincible energy and of extraordinary discrimination and skill in the treatment of the class of cases that come before the Charity Organization workers. She rested from her labors Dec. 24, 1891.

Jacobs. — Denver mourns the loss in 1892 of Mrs. Frances Jacobs, who so won the confidence and esteem of that entire community that at her obsequies the city stood still while Christians, Catholic, and Protestant alike vied with her fellow-Hebrews in loving honors to her memory; and a hospital that bears her name was established by popular contributions, as her monument.

It would be a grateful task to linger over these tributes to the memories of departed colleagues who live still in our esteem, but time forbids. These were, among many others we would name did space permit, by priority of labors or by eminence of influence, men and women of so wide note that their names could not be passed in silence. Others have wrought with no less consecration of heart, no less generosity of thought and hand. Gratitude for the inspiration of their example, for the quickening touch of their noble personality, follows them beyond the tomb. We love to think of these souls, so radiant here with pure charity, having done their humane work to the least of these His brethren, as having entered into the joy of their Lord.

CHARLES D. KELLOGG, New York, *Chairman,*
P. W. AYRES, Cincinnati,
T. GUILFORD SMITH, Buffalo,
J. W. WALK, M.D., Philadelphia,
W. R. WALPOLE, Portland, Ore.,

Of the Committee.

APPENDIX A.

CHARITY ORGANIZATION SOCIETIES IN NORTH AMERICA.

In Correspondence with each other as Occasion arises.

UNITED STATES.

DATE OF ORG'N.	CITY OR TOWN.	NAME.	LOCATION.	CORRESPONDING OFFICER.
1883.	Albany, N.Y.	Charity Organization Society.	8 Douw's Buildings.	John Moir, Gen. Sec.
1890.	Auburn, Me.	Associated Charities.	53 Drummond St.	Miss Ruth Caswell, Sec.
1881.	Baltimore, Md.	Charity Organization Society.	12 Wil-on Building.	Miss M. E. Richmond, Gen. Sec.
1846.	Bangor, Me.	Associated Charities.	9 Hayward St.	Mrs. Frances H. Noble, Sec.
1885.	Binghamton, N.Y.	Bureau of Associated Charities.	96 Chenango St.	Mrs. J. H. Barnes, Sec. and Treas.
1879.	Boston, Mass.	Associated Charities.	41 Charity Building	Miss Z. D. Smith, Gen. Sec.
1886.	Bridgeport, Conn.	Associated Charities.	218 Main Street.	Mrs. H. E. Raymond, Cor. Sec.
1878.	Brooklyn, N.Y.	Bureau of Charities.	69 Schermerhorn St.	
1877.	Buffalo, N.Y.	Charity Organization Society.	Fitch Institute, 165 Swan St.	Nathaniel S. Rosenau, Gen. Sec. and Treas.
1885.	Burlington, Iowa.	Charity Organization Society.	502 Jefferson St., Room 2.	Miss M. E. Starr, Sec.
1881.	Cambridge, Mass.	Associated Charities.	Central Sq.	Miss S. A. Pear, Registrar.
1884.	Castleton, S.I., N.Y.	Charity Organization Society.	62 Jersey St., New Brighton.	Miss Ford, Sec.
1888.	Charleston, S.C.	Associated Charities Society.	Mills House, Meeting St.	Mrs. M. A. Rhett, Sec.
1883.	Chattanooga, Tenn.	Associated Charities.	731 Chestnut St.	W. J. Trimble, Supt.
1879.	Cincinnati, Ohio.	Associated Charities.	45 East 5th St.	Philip W. Ayres, Gen. Sec.
1881.	Cleveland, Ohio.	Bethel Associated Charities.	309 Spring St.	Henry N. Raymond, Supt.
	Clinton, Mass.	Associated Charities.		Mrs. Edward L. Green, Sec.
1886.	Davenport, Iowa.	Associated Charities.	115 West 6th St.	Mrs. Nettie F. Howard, Agent
1889.	Decatur Ill.	Industrial and Charitable Union.		Miss E. M. Whitehurst, Sec.
1889.	Denver, Col.	Charity Organization Society.	Room 32, Court House.	Mrs. Izetta George, Registrar.
1890.	Detroit, Mich.	Association of Charities.	35 East Congress St.	Dr. Jas. A. Post, Gen. Sec.
1881.	District of Columbia.	Charity Organization Society	In suspense.	
1884.	Fall River, Mass.	Associated Charities.	60 North Main St.	Miss Alice E. Wetherbee, Agent.
1890.	Hartford, Conn.	Charity Organization Society	2 Grove St.	George B. Thayer, Supt.
1879.	Indianapolis, Ind.	Charity Organization Society.	Room 1, Plymouth Building	James Smith, Gen. Sec.
1886.	Janesville, Wis.	Associated Charities.	Jackman's Block.	
1891.	Lexington, Ky.	Charity Organization Society		Mrs. Walter Scott, Pres.
1891.	Lincoln, Neb.	Charity Organization Society.	134 South 12th St.	Mrs. Annie McCormick, Agent.
1891.	Lockport, N.Y	Charity Organization Society.	12 Y. M. C. A. Building.	

DATE OF ORGIN.	CITY OR TOWN.	NAME.	LOCATION.	CORRESPONDING OFFICER.
1884.	Louisville, Ky.	Charity Organization Society.	221 East Walnut St.	Mrs. George Deering, Gen Sec.
1887.	Lynn, Mass.	Associated Charities	Lee Hall, Room 5, 10 City Hall Sq.	Miss Alice S. Taylor, Registrar
1889.	Mansfield, Ohio.	Mansfield Humane Society.	King Building, Park Ave, West.	A. G. Thornton, Supt.
1884.	Marietta, Ohio.	Associated Charities.	4th St.	Wm. R. Buck, Rec. Sec.
1881.	Milwaukee, Wis.	Associated Charities.	416 Milwaukee St.	Howland Russel, Sec.
1884.	Minneapolis, Minn.	Associated Charities.	23 South 4th St.	George D. Holt, Sec.
1882.	Newark, N. J.	Bureau of Associated Charities	222 Market St.	J. Huyler Smith, Supt.
1884	New Brunswick, N. J.	Charity Organization Society.	Free Public Library.	Miss Mary Gordon Shand, Agent.
1886.	Newburg, N. Y.	Associated Charities.	65 Water St.	Mrs. Mary G. Wood, Supt.
1878.	New Haven, Conn.	Organized Charities Association.	200 Orange St.	Sherwood O. Preston, Agent.
1883.	New Orleans, La.	Conference of Charities.	223 St. Joseph St.	Miss Corinne Folger, Registrar.
1879.	Newport, R.I.	Charity Organization Society.	301½ Thames St.	Mrs. K. A. Curtis, Sec. and Agent.
1888.	Newton, Mass.	Associated Charities.	Newtonville Sq.	Mrs. M. R. Martin, Sec. and Agent.
1881.	New York City.	Charity Organization Society.	United Charities Building.	Charles D. Kellogg, Gen. Sec.
1888.	Oakland, Cal.	Associated Charities.	418 Tenth St.	Newton Sewell, Gen. Supt.
1887.	Omaha, Neb.	Associated Charities.	807 Howard St.	H. M. James, Gen. Sec.
1878	Orange, N.J.	Bureau of Associated Charities.	65 Essex Ave.	Miss Jennie Fancher, Agent.
1889.	Pasadena, Cal.	Charity Organization Society.	7 North Fair Oaks Ave.	Annie L. Bartlett, Sec.
1884.	Pawtucket, R.I.	Associated Charities.	3 Dorrance Building, 175 Main St.	Graham Cowperthwaite, Agent.
1878.	Philadelphia, Pa.	Society for Organizing Charity.	1705 Chestnut St.	Dr. James W. Walk, Gen. Sec.
1879.	Portland, Me.	Associated Charities.	Room 9, City Building	Miss Celia M. Patten, Sec. and Treas.
1888.	Portland, Ore.	City Board of Charities.	213 Fourth St.	William R. Warpole, Sec.
1879.	Poughkeepsie, N.Y.	Charity Organization Society.	8 Cannon St.	Thomas L. Wing, 7 Garden St.
1892.	Providence, R.I.	Society for Organizing Charity.	128 North Main St	Eli Whitney Blake, Jr., Gen Manager.
1880.	Richmond, Ind.	Associated Charities.	109 North 12th St.	Mrs. Anna M. Starr, Sec.
1890.	Rochester, N.Y.	Charity Organization Society.	87 South Washington St.	Miss Helen D. Arnold, Sec. and Treas.
1885.	Saginaw, E.S., Mich.	Associated Charities.	100 Ward St.	Mrs Emma Bronson, Sec.
1892.	St. Paul, Minn.	Associated Charities.	141 East 9th St.	James F. Jackson, Gen. Sec.
1891.	Salem, Mass.	Associated Charities.	175 Essex St.	Miss Anna C. Cross, Registrar.
1881.	Salem, N.J.	Society for Organizing Charity.	121 West Broadway.	Miss Anna H. Van Meter, Sec
1888.	San Francisco, Cal.	Associated Charities.	425 Pine St.	Arthur G. Smiley, Registrar.
1885.	Springfield, Ohio.	Bureau of Labor and Charities.	West County Building.	H. H. Cumback, Supt.
1878.	Syracuse, N.Y.	Provident Association.	4 Hendricks Block.	Charles de B. Mills, Gen. Sec.
1880.	Tarrytown, N.Y.	Associated Charities.		Mrs. W. H. Moore, Sec.
1881.	Taunton, Mass.	Society for Organizing Charity.	Historical Hall.	Miss Charlotte L. Peckham, Supt
1892.	Terre Haute, Ind	Charity Organization Society.	501½ Ohio St.	W. C. Smallwood, Gen. Sec.
1891.	Tivoli, N.Y.	Society for Organizing Charity.	Madalin, N.Y.	Miss Kate Ferree, Sec.
1883.	Washington, D.C.	Associated Charities.	116 West State St.	Miss M. M. Johnson, Sec.
1881.	Watertown, N.Y.	Bureau of Charities.	811 G St., N.W.	L. S. Emery, Gen. Sec.
1883.	Wilmington, Del	Associated Charities.	22 Stone St.	Mrs. L. C. Walker, Sec. and Agent.
1884.	Worcester, Mass.	Associated Charities.	837 Tatnall St.	Mrs. Mary A. T. Clark, Supt.
1890.	Yonkers, N.Y.	Charity Organization Society.	35 Pearl St.	Mrs. Eliza J. Lee, Gen. Sec.
1883.			3 Post-office Building.	George Rayner, Jr., Sec.

Appendix A.— *Concluded.*

The following Relief Societies have partly adapted Charity Organization Principles, and correspond with the Foregoing.

DATE OF ORG'N.	CITY OR TOWN.	NAME.	LOCATION.	CORRESPONDING OFFICER.
1884.	Bryn Mawr, Pa.	Citizens' Association.		Walter Bevan, Sec. and Treas.
1884.	Camden, N.J.	Society for Prevention and Relief of Poverty.		
1872.	Chicago, Ill.	Relief and Aid Society.	725 Federal St.	Abel Smith, Supt.
1890.	Colorado Springs, Col.	Ladies' Aid Society.	61 La Salle St.	Rev. C. G. Trusdell.
1876.	Fitchburg, Mass.	Benevolent Union.	Room 22, Bank Building.	Miss Louisa Schnapp, Agent
1892.	Flushing, N.Y.	United Workers.	Room 50, Dickinson's Block, Main St.	Miss Alice Miller, Agent
1890.	Kansas City, Mo.	Provident Association.	66 Locust St.	G. L. Gordon, Sec.
1859.	Lawrence, Mass.	City Mission.	723 East 9th St.	Nicholas W. Casey, Sec.
1887.	Madison, Wis.	Benevolent Society.	206 Essex St.	Rev. Clark Carter, Sec. and City Missionary.
1875.	Malden, Mass.	Industrial Aid Society.	23 East Main St.	O. S. Norsman, Sec.
1875.	Pittsburg, Pa.	Ass'n Improv'g Condition of Poor.	76 Sixth Ave.	W. H. Sargent, Treas.
1878.	Pittsfield, Mass.	Union for Home Work.	29 Dunham St.	Mrs. S. E. Lippincott, Supt. and Sec.
1878.	Plainfield, N.J.	Relief Association.	45 West 24 St.	
1881.	Pueblo, Col.	Benevolent Union.	223 Victoria Ave.	Miss Anna J. Pray, Supt.
1872.	Seattle, Wash.	Board of Friendly Visitors.		Joanna S. Sperry, Pres. and Manager.
1877.	St. Louis, Mo.	Provident Association.	1820 Madison St.	Mrs. Charles F. Fishback, Pres.
1876.	Springfield, Mass.	Union Relief Association.	7 City Hall.	W. J. Clark Supt.
1892.	Waterbury, Conn.	Directors of Christian Visitation and Charity.	77 Kingsbury St.	James H. Lewis, Sec.

DOMINION OF CANADA.

DATE OF ORG'N.	CITY OR TOWN.	NAME.	LOCATION.	CORRESPONDING OFFICER.
	Toronto.	St. George's Society.	7 Louisa St.	Rev. Horace George Hoadley, Supt.
1884.	Halifax.	Ass'n Improv'g Condition of Poor.	61 Granville St.	

APPENDIX B.

CITY.	POPULATION, 1880.	YEAR OF FORMATION.
Baltimore,	332,213	1881
Boston,	362,535	1879
Brooklyn,	566,663	1879
Buffalo,	176,607	1877
Cambridge,	52,669	1881
Cincinnati,	255,139	1879
Cleveland,	160,146	1881
Detroit,	185,000	1880
Indianapolis,	75,056	1879
Milwaukee,	175,000	1881
Newark,	136,000	1882
New Haven,	60,000	1878
Newport, R.I.,	15,693	1879
New York,	1,300,000	1882
Orange, N.J.,	13,207	1878
Philadelphia,	843,000	1878
Portland, Me.,	33,810	1879
Poughkeepsie,	20,207	1879
Salem, N.J.,	5,056	1881
Syracuse,	51,792	1878
Taunton, Mass.,	21,213	1881
Washington, D.C.,	177,624	1881
	5,069,330	

AFFILIATED SOCIETIES.

CITY.	POPULATION, 1880.	YEAR OF FORMATION
Chicago,	503,185	1872
Fitchburg, Mass.,	12,429	1876
Kansas City,	55,785	1880
Lawrence, Mass.,	41,000	1859
Malden, Mass.,	12,017	1875
Pittsburg,	156,389	1875
Pittsfield, Mass.,	13,364	1878
Plainfield, N.J.,	81,125	1878
Pueblo, Col.,	3,217	1881
St. Louis, Mo.,	350,518	1877
Springfield, Mass.,	33,340	1876
	1,262,369	

APPENDIX C

POPULATION, 4,866,550. NOT RELIEF GIVERS.	POPULATION, 2,998,950. RELIEF GIVERS.	POPULATION, 714,650. EMERGENT RELIEF GIVERS.
Albany, N.Y.	*Bryn Mawr, Pa.	Auburn, Me.
Baltimore.	Cleveland, Ohio.	Bangor, Me.
Boston.	*Kansas City, Mo.	Bridgeport, Conn.
Brooklyn, N.Y.	*Lawrence, Mass.	Buffalo.
Burlington, Ia.	*Malden, Mass.	Davenport, Ia.
Castleton, S.I., N.Y.	New Haven, Conn.	Minneapolis.
Charleston, S.C.	Newton, Mass.	Newburg, N.Y.
Cincinnati.	Pasadena, Cal.	Omaha.
Detroit.	Pawtucket. R.I.	Pueblo, Cal.
Hartford.	Philadelphia.	
Indianapolis.	Richmond, Ind.	
Lincoln, Neb.	Salem, N.J.	
Lynn, Mass.	Springfield, Ohio.	
Newark, N.J.	Taunton, Mass.	
New Brunswick, N.J.	Tivoli, N.Y.	
Newport, R.I.	Trenton, N.J.	
New York City.	Waterbury, Conn.	
Orange, N.J.	Wilmington, Del.	
Plainfield.	Worcester, Mass.	
Portland, Me.	Yonkers, N.Y.	
Providence, R.I.		
Rochester, N.Y.		
Salem, Mass.		
Seattle, Wash.		
Syracuse, N.Y.		

APPENDIX D.

The following is a schedule of questions submitted to each of the related Societies upon the replies of which this report is based.

Answers were requested where practicable for the year 1882 (or the first year of the organization of each), and for 1892 for purposes of comparison, as the several tables will show.

I. PRELIMINARY.

1. Location of your Society; 2. Its legal name; 3. Date of organization, date of incorporation; 4. Local conditions which led to the formation of your Society; *a.* did it spring up independently, or was it initiated by older charitable organizations? *b.* state of legal administration of relief at that time (1. outdoor; 2. indoor); *c.* state of voluntary charity at the time; 5. Do you distribute alms from your own funds? 6. By what methods do you disseminate your views and principles, in order to gain adherents or improve the practice of others? 7. What do you publish in the way of periodicals? give titles; of occasional papers? give titles.

II. ORGANIZATION.

1. Number of unpaid administrative officers: *a.* men; *b.* women; 2. Number of paid officers and agents: *a.* men; *b.* women: 3. Number of Friendly Visitors, voluntary workers and teachers: *a.* men; *b.* women; 4. Number of branch or district organizations controlled by your society; 5. Conferences, by Committees or Boards, concerning treatment of applicants; 6. Number of your contributors: *a.* individuals; *b.* associations or churches; *c.* amount received from municipal authorities; 7. Amount of your income; 8. Amount of invested funds; 9. Average number of cases assigned to Friendly Visitors.

III. LINES OF WORK DEVELOPED.

(*State number of instances or cases.*)

1. *Repression.*— a. Treatment of vagrants: (*a*) number turned over to police, (*b*) number lodged by your Society, (*c*) number employed in wood-yard or other like test places, (*d*) street beggars and impostors suppressed; b. fraudulent societies detected.

2. *Co-operation.*—a With municipal or State boards: number in your town, number co-operating; b. with societies and institutions of relief (*e.g.*, relief societies, hospitals, orphanages, etc.): number in your town, number co-operating; c. with churches: number in your town, number co-operating; d. with individuals: population of town, number co-operating; e. to what extent (percentage) have you secured registration from (*a*) public official relief? (*b*) voluntary societies? (*c*) churches? (*d*) private charitable institutions? f. number of cases investigated for others.

3. *Provident Schemes in your City.*—a. Crèches, or nurseries: number of inmates; b. kindergartens; c. industrial training, as sewing, cooking, trade schools: (*a*) nat-

ure of, (*b*) number of, (*c*) beneficiaries of; d. savings funds: (*a*) number of depositors, (*b*) amount of deposits; e. co-operative beneficial societies: (*a*) nature of, (*b*) members of.

4. *Sanitary Work.*—a. Tenements improved through landlords or through changed habits; b. removal to better quarters; c. open-air excursions: number of beneficiaries; d. country homes secured; temporary outing; permanent.

5. *Other Agencies inaugurated and managed by your Society.*—a. Nature of; b. number of beneficiaries.

IV. RESULTS.

1. Number of cases treated: a. accounted worthy of continuous relief (*i.e.*, orphans, aged, permanently disabled); b. worthy of temporary aid (*i.e.*, sick, injured, overtaken by emergency); c. accounted to need work rather than alms; d. not cases for relief: (*a*) because of having means or relatives able to provide for them, (*b*) because of vicious habits, imposture, shiftlessness; 2. Disposition made of cases: a. cases not taken in charge: (*a*) placed in institutions, (*b*) put in complete charge of churches or societies, (*c*) turned over to police; b. cases assumed for treatment: (*a*) aid procured from municipal or State relief boards, (*b*) aid procured from churches or societies, (*c*) aid procured from individuals, (*d*) aided by loans, (*e*) employment secured, (*f*) applicant's own resources adequately developed, (*g*) removed to care of relatives or new situations, (*h*) estimate of number brought to self-maintenance.

V. ANALYSIS.

(*From National Statistical Blanks.*)

Social State.— Married couples, widows, deserted wives, single women, deserted husbands or widowers, single men, orphaned or abandoned children, divorced or separated (legally), adult brother and sister as one family.

Number and Ages.— Under 14, 14 to 20, 20 to 40, 40 to 55, 55 to 70, over 70, total number in family.

Nativity of Heads of Families.— United States, white; United States, colored; British-American, white; British-American, colored; Dutch, English, French, and Belgian, German, Italian, Irish, Polish, and Russian, Scandinavian, Scotch, and Welsh, Spanish, and Portuguese, Swiss, other countries.

Education of Heads of Families.— Can read and write; can read, not write; cannot read or write.

VI. OBSERVATIONS.

1. What changes of policy or method has your society made in its history? 2. What improvement in the condition of the dependent or alms-seeking poor has been achieved under the local observation of your society? 3. What improvement has been made in the administration of relief, either municipal or voluntary? 4. What phases of your work have been satisfactory? 5. What improvements of method do you think most desirable? 6. What local publications do you know of beyond your own on scientific charity? a. collegiate; b. university; c. State or political; d. general.

City or Town.	Inu
	18⸻
Albany	⸻
Auburn, Me...............	...
Baltimore	⸻
Bangor, Me.................. ⸻......	..
Boston	1,6⸻
Bridgeport, Conn	....
Brooklyn, N. Y.	⸻
Bryn Mawr........	..
Buffalo	...
Burlington Iowa.....................	....
Castleton, S. I., N Y.........	....
Charleston, S. C.....................	
Cincinnati..........	9⸻
Cleveland..............................	....
Davenport, Iowa.........	....
Denver, Col.....	....
Detroit............................	....
Hartford, Conn	....
Indianapolis........................	
Kansas City, Mo.............	1⸻
Lawrence, Mass	..
Lincoln, Neb	..
Lynn	..
Milwaukee........	....
Minneapolis....	....
Newark, N. J	⸻
New Brunswick....	..
Newburg, N. Y......................	....
New Haven, Conn	1⸻
Newport, R. 1......	....
Newton, Mass................	....
New York City..	3⸻
Omaha...................	....
Orange, N. J.................... . ..	⸻
Pasadena, Cal	...
Pawtucket, R. I.............	.⸻
Philadelphia.....	*1⸻
Plainfield, N. J....	1⸻
Portland, Me........	...
Portland, Ore.......................	...
Providence, R. 1	...
Rochester, N. Y....................	....
Salem, Mass....................... ..	..
Salem, N. J	....
San Francisco, Cal....	....
Seattle, Wash....	....
Syracuse, N. Y...	⸻
Taunton, Mass	4⸻
Tivoli, N. Y	...
Trenton, N. J....	....
Waterbury, Conn	...
Wilmington, Del	.. ..
Worcester, Mass........	....
Yonkers, N. Y., report of 1891	..
	3,8⸻

1 These figures include only contribu⸻
whom no account is returned.
2 Contributors to Ward Associations

APPENDIX E.

FINANCE.

CITY OR TOWN	CONTRIBUTORS						INCOME			INVESTED FUNDS
	INDIVIDUALS		ASSOCIATIONS or CHURCHES		FROM CITY OR STATE					
	1892	1893	1892	1893	1892	1893	1892	1893	1893	1893
Albany	74	203		....			$600 00	$1,032 00		
Auburn Me.....		22		Yes				330 00		$190 00
Baltimore	..	614		»			1 315 00	6 806 00		1,000 00
Bangor, Me				4				102 41		
Boston	1,681	1,284	74	16	....		11,392 63	17,444 36		$2,000 00
Bridgeport, Conn										11,000 00 in Building
Brooklyn, N. Y	50	2,640		Yes		$1 013 54	2,025 93	20 033 00		
Bryn Mawr . .								('91) 580 00		
Buffalo		155					1,413 00	6 431 57		
Burlington Iowa		50						107 00		$800,973 00
Charleston, S. L. N Y		53					......	100 90		
Charleston, S. C .		175					......	855 00		
Cincinnati	250	677		5			11,966 23	8,151 71		5,000 00
Cleveland		400		5				100 00		
Davenport, Iowa....		152		1	......	1		8,000 00		
Denver, Col.....		503				10,000 00		23,000 00		
Detroit		250					...	2,500 00		
Hartford, Conn . .		112						1,000 00		
Indianapolis		489					1,300 00	6 025 00		
Kansas City, Mo......	141	212	7			$575 00	2,215 59	6,002 66		
Lawrence, Mass			28	34		Free rent	2,584 48	3,050 35		
Lincoln, Neb		264		21				888 07		
Lynn		80		3			......	1 100 00		1,025 00
Milwaukee.... . .		600	11				2,450 00	3 100 00		
Minneapolis		500		2				6,500 00		750 00
Newark, N. J	72	550					2,160 00	3 360 00		700 00
New Brunswick . .		62	....					330 00		
Newburg, N. Y		195						1,201 85		58 50
New Haven, Conn	125	197	10	12			2,018 30	4,705 00		5,504 00
Newport, R. I								1,090 00		
Newton, Mass ...	......	300						836 00		
New York City .	384	2,374	4	81			$5,597 00	40 920 00		41,254 00 + . shai in Charities Build ing. $130,000
Omaha		600						4,800 00		
Orange, N. J	70	326	8				910 10	1,124 17		
Pasadena, Cal			1					630 71		
Pawtucket, R. I		150						1,840 00		500 00
Philadelphia.....	*150	*432				*$4,875 00	*24,187 36	67,880 95		
Plainfield, N. J....	141	132		Yes	$617	680 00	2,103 81	2,391 83		
Portland, Me						250 00	......			
Portland, Ore		875						7,723 05		
Providence, R. I								2,000 00		
Rochester, N. Y		250						2,000 00		
Salem, Mass........		107						1,000 00		400 00
Salem, N. J		8		8			219 50	252 00		
San Francisco, Cal....		248						4,180 00		
Seattle, Wash	......	350						2,500 00		
Syracuse, N. Y	58	142						2,548 35		
Taunton, Mass ..	40	41	8	9		700 00		500 00		
Tivoli, N. Y. ...		86						900 00		
Trenton, N. J....		291						2,112 50		
Waterbury, Conn ..		83		7						
Wilmington, Del		106		2				4,667 4..		
Worcester Mass		107		2		75 00				
Yonkers, N. Y , report of 1891		23						809 46		
	3,839	15,720	79	313	$617	$17,677 54	$96,019 50	$355,421 80		$406,402 75
		700.8*↓		207.6*↓				208.2*↓		

¹ These figures include only contributors to the Central Treasury, and not the hundreds of contributors to the Ward Associations, of whom no account is returned.
² Contributors to Ward Associations only The contributions to the Central Treasury not returned, but probably about $15 00

CITY OR TOWN.	ADMINISTRATIVE OFFICERS.			
	Men.		Women	
	1882	1892	1882	189
Albany..............	4	4	......	...
Auburn, Me..........	......	......	......	...
Baltimore, Md.....	11	41	......	
Bangor, Me	......	......		
Boston, Mass.........	87	94	117	18
Bridgeport, Conn......	......	......	......	
Brooklyn, N. Y.... ...	..	...	. ...	..
Bryn Mawr, Pa........	......	...	......	'.
Buffalo, N. Y..........	43	51	.....	2
Burlington, Ia..	....	2	......	
Castleton, S. I., N. Y...	......	......	.. .	1
Charleston, S. C.....	... ...	......		
Cincinnati, O..........	21	13	24	1
Cleveland, O..........	.. ...	29	......	
Davenport, Ia..	......	19	......	
Denver, Col..........	......	*13	......	.,
Detroit, Mich..........	.....	3	......	. ,
Hartford, Conn	......	40	......	
Indianapolis, Ind......	40	30	......	1
Lawrence, Mass........	. ...	60	...	..
Lincoln, Neb..........	......	22	......	
Lynn, Mass..........	......	5	......	
Milwaukee, Wis.	28	31	1	
Minneapolis, Minn. ...	......	5	......	...
Newark, N. J	15	30	4	
New Brunswick, N. J..	.....	13	......	1
Newburg, N. Y.... ..	......	8	......	1
New Haven, Conn.....	17	41	4	
Newport, R. I.........	10	13	4	
Newton, Mass.........	......	12	......	
New York City...	21	54	2	
Omaha, Neb..	.....	......	....	..
Orange, N. J..........	......	......	......	
Pawtucket, R. I.......	......	7	.. ..	1
Philadelphia, Pa......	......	34	......	
Plainfield, N. J	......	23	......	2
Portland, Me..........	......	......	......	
Portland, Ore...... ..	......	9	......	...
Providence, R. I.......	......	......	.. ..	...
Pueblo, Col	......	7	1	2
Richmond, Ind	......	......	.. .	2
Rochester, N. Y.......	......	3	......	
Salem, Mass..........	......	5	......	
Salem, N. J	......	......	3	
San Francisco, Cal.....	......	12	......	2
Seattle, Wash.........	......	......	...	..
Syracuse, N. Y......	......	9	....	
Taunton, Mass........	......	14	......	
Tivoli, N. Y	......	......	......	1
Trenton, N. J	......	......	......	
Waterbury, Conn.,....	......	5	......	..
Wilmington, Del......	......	12	.. ..	1
Worcester, Mass.	...	......	......	...
Total.....	297	763	160	51
Increase..... ...	......	156.92	......	219

* No distinction of sex made in the return
women where the returns make no distinction

N. B.—Examination of these figures will
of the answers required. Conferences on C
the figures are exact multiples or divisors o
dently refer to the number of branch or di
sult would be misleading.

ORGANIZATION.

City or Town.	Administrative Officers.				Paid Officers or Agents.				Friendly Visitors.				Average Cases to Visitor.		Branch or District Organizations.		Conferences on Cases.	
	Men.		Women.		Men.		Women.		Men.		Women.							
	1891	1892	1891	1892	1891	1892	1891	1892	1891	1892	1891	1892	1891	1892	1891	1892	1891	1892
Albany	4	4			1	1				6			23					
Auburn, Me.						1							34	15				
Baltimore, Md.	11	11		8	1		2	11		41			195	5	1	8	1	9
Bangor, Me				5							11		18	4				21
Boston, Mass	87	94	117	196	8		11	21		84	*612	683	101	3	14	15	164	164
Bridgeport, Conn				6							60							11
Brooklyn, N. Y.					1	1	1	6		113		*512						12
Bryn Mawr, Pa.						3						17						3
Buffalo, N. Y.	44	51		98	2	5		2				12		1	2	3	2	3
Burlington, Ia.		2		2				1				*70						3
Castleton, S. I., N. Y				12				1				46		2		3		
Charleston, S. C.								1				12						
Cincinnati, O.	21	13	24	15	5	6	4	3	10	70	85	145			11	1		6
Cleveland, O.		26		5		2		2				*79						
Davenport, Ia		19		9				2										2
Denver, Col.		*13				1		3		30		90		5		16		53
Detroit, Mich.		3				2				60		75						
Hartford, Conn		60		4		2												12
Indianapolis, Ind	40	30		16	1	1	1	5				80						50
Lawrence Mass.		66				1						90						
Lincoln, Neb		24		3		2						45						12
Lyns, Mass		5		7				1				23						2
Milwaukee, Wis	20	31	1	5	1	1	1	1							3	3	4	12
Minneapolis, Minn		5				1		3		2		96		1	50	4	4	42
Newark, N. J.	16	30	4	4	1	1	4	5			75	100	87	87	2	3	2	3
New Brunswick, N. J		13		13			4	1			*16	*50	1	25	6	3	7	4
Newburg, N. Y.		8		14				1				25						
New Haven, Conn	17	41	4	6	2	2	1	1		4		7	18	2				102
Newport, R. I.	10	18	4	5			1	1		9		13						96
Newton, Mass		12		9				1			17	29						
New York City	21	64	2	8	4	9	6	31			235	218		6	10		6	
Omaha, Neb						3				5		135						
Orange, N. J.						1					34	60						
Pawtucket, R. I.		7		14		1						64						
Philadelphia, Pa.		54		2		14		15						9				
Plainfield, N. J		28		25	1	1	1	1			50	51	1	3	21	17		62
Portland, Me.								1			80	30		8				
Portland, Ore		9				3		1		15		25			5			
Providence, R. I.						1		1										
Pueblo, Col		7	1					1		7	9	19						
Richmond, Ind.				23				1										
Rochester, N. Y.		3		1				3				100		1		3		8
Salem, Mass		5		4				1				51	1	1				8
Salem, N. J.			3	1				1			33	25		1				11
San Francisco, Cal.		19		25				2				12						27
Seattle, Wash.												107		2				36
Syracuse, N. Y		9		2	1	2	1	1		31								
Taunton, Mass		11		8				1				18						
Tivoli, N. Y				10														
Trenton, N. J				4				1				13						52
Waterbury, Conn		5				2				2		91		2				6
Wilmington, Del		12		13				2		2		95		5	6			6
Worcester, Mass								3		3		85		2				
Total	217	768	160	531	24	77	36	135	10	456	1729	8554		97		300		
Increase		156.9%		219.1%		221%		275%		14%		163.9%						
								933.3%		9.8%								

* No distinction of sex made in the returns. In this table administrative officers have been credited to men and Friendly Visitors to women where the returns make no distinction, because these are the sexes that predominate in those sorts of service.

N. B. Examination of these figures will show that the correspondents by whom they were supplied varied greatly in their conceptions of the answers required. Conferences on Cases refers to meetings of officers and visitors to consider treatment of applicants. Where the figures are exact multiples or divisors of 12 and 52, they indicate monthly and weekly conferences. In some instances the figures evidently refer to the number of branch or district associations holding conferences. The columns are not added to a total where the result would be misleading.

Newark, N. J.	New Brunswick, N. J.	Newburg, N. Y.	New Haven.	Newport, R. I.	Newton. Mass.	New York.	Omaha.	Philadelphia.	Plainfield, N. J.	Portland, Ore.	Providence, R. I.	Rochester, N. Y.	Salem, Mass.	Salem. N J	San Francisco.	Seattle, Wash.	Syracuse.	Waterbury, Conn.
			56			318				7					22	23		1
			3009				620	15476		206		30			22	150	32	11
			2281			Est. 2800		979		116		45		23·13	163			8
			42			Est. 350				5				1	3	56	55	12
			5			55									1			..
1	1	1	4	1		11					1	2	1	1		2	2	1
1	1	1	4	1		11					1	2	1	1		2	2	1
52	8	6	13			350	10			29		40				5	10	4
49	6	6	13			121	10		3	16	All hospitals.	40		2	85	5		4
127	23 Common.	22	68	21	35	590	76	25		60	60	92		12	150	20	73	15
114	21		68		17	367	40	25		33	22	90		8	19	19		10
							142000											35000
						2000	1200											167
100%		Partial.	90%	100%		100%						25%	100%		50%	100%	100%	Conside-rable.
			90%			90%					75%	40%	50%		10%	60%		
ost.			25%			80%					35%	20%			25%	40%		
100%			75%			70%					15%	15%				25%		
100%	18					2172	500				102	20			1758	145	77	52
						41										27		
						Est. 30										13		
2500		500				1770			13	6170		101						
160								Co-opera-tion.						41		11		1
						7										35	42	
	Clubs and reading rooms.	First Aid to Injured.				Wood yard, Laundry, Penny Bank.		Wood yard, Wayfarers' Lodges.								Wood yard.		Broom shop, work test.

APPENDIX L.

BIBLIOGRAPHY OF THE CHARITY ORGANIZATION SOCIETIES OF THE UNITED STATES.

BALTIMORE.

Directory of Charitable and Beneficent Organizations, 1892, 16mo, 2d edition, 141 pp.; The Charities Record, a periodical succeeding the Confidential Circular; Annual Reports of the Charity Organization Society of Baltimore; Charities; The Relation of the State, the City, and the Individual to Modern Philanthropic Work. A. G. Warner, Ph.D.; Report of a Conference on Charities held in Baltimore, April, 1887, published by the Baltimore Charity Organization Society, 1887, Charity Organization Society Pr.M.; The Needs of Self-supporting Women, Clare de Graffenried; Work among Workingwomen in Baltimore. H. B. Adams, Ph.D.; Philanthropy, Richard T. Ely; Relations of Private and Public to Organized Charity, W. F. Slocum; Notes on Literature of Charities, Professor Adams; Ashrott's Poor Relief in the United States (translation); Extracts from International Congress at Paris (translation); Education of the Friendly Visitor, Zilpha D. Smith; A Few Words to Fresh Visitors, Octavia Hill.

BOSTON.

Directory of Charitable Organizations, 1891, 12mo, 3d edition, 351 pp.; Annual Reports; Charity Organization, by Robert Treat Paine, 14 pp.; Essays by Octavia Hill, 34 pp.; Relation of Private Almsgivers to the Associated Charities, 1 p.; Work of Volunteer Visitors, by Robert Treat Paine, 19 pp.; An Appeal for Help and Workers; Hints to a Conference; Circular to Visitors concerning Drunkenness; The District Conference and its Executive Committee; Directions for the Work of an Agent; The Work of the Central Office; Sending New Applicants to the Overseers of the Poor; The Old Charity and the New, by H. L. Wayland, D.D., For Visitors of the Associated Charities; Laws applying to Tenements in the City of Boston; more than a score of papers now out of print.

BUFFALO.

Handbook of Charity Organization, by Rev. S. H. Gurteen, 254 pp.; Hints and Suggestions to Visitors of the Poor, by the same; Phases of Charity, by the same; Provident Schemes, by the same; What is Charity Organization? by the same.

CLEVELAND.

The Journal and Bulletin, a weekly paper representing the benevolent organizations of the city.

INDIANAPOLIS.

Annual Year Book of Charities ; Reprints of papers by Octavia Hill, S. H. Gurteen, Oscar C. McCulloch, C. S. Loch, and Francis Wayland

NEW YORK.

New York Charities Directory of the Charitable and Beneficent Societies and Institutions of the City, 5th edition, 472 pp., 16mo, $1, to paid officers of churches and societies 50 cents; The Charities Review, a Journal of Practical Sociology, yearly subscription (8 numbers) $1 ; Work of Friendly Visitors, 1 p.; On District Conferences, by Mrs. James T. Fields, 4 pp.; Inaugural Paper of Organizing Secretary, 4 pp.; Cold Victuals, by Hon. Charles S. Fairchild, 2 pp.; How to repress Pauperism, by Robert Treat Paine, 16 pp.; Official vs. Private Relief, a reprint from London Charity Organization Society Reporter, 2 pp.; Duties of Friendly Visitors, by Mrs. C. R. Lowell, 4 pp.; The Pauper Question, by D. O. Kellogg, 18 pp.; Profits and Possibilities of the Proper Organization of Charity, by Hon. A. S. Hewitt, 8 pp.; The Old Charity and the New, by Rev. H. L. Wayland, D.D., 4 pp.; Philanthropy, by Richard T. Ely, Ph.D., 8 pp.; The Charity Organization Idea, by Ansley Wilcox, 4 pp.; How to adapt Charity Organization Methods to Small Communities, by Mrs. Charles R. Lowell, 8 pp.; The Wastes of Charity, Rt. Rev. Henry C. Potter, D.D., 8 pp.; Methods of Organization of Charity, by Alexander Johnston, 8 pp.; General Suggestions for the Treatment of Different Classes of Cases, 8 pp.; What We ask Co-operating Societies to do for Us, and What We are ready to do for Them, 2 pp.; Friendly Visiting, by Mrs. James J. Putnam, 8 pp.; The Savings Society, by Mrs. John H. Scribner, 8 pp.; The Church in Charity, by Alexander Johnston, 8 pp.; The Elberfeld System, a reprint from the Hospital, 8 pp.; Drunkards' Families, by Rev. W. F. Slocum, 6 pp.; Charity Organization and the Church, by Rev. Henry Van Dyke, D.D.; Report of Special Committee on Immigration, by Professor Richmond M. Smith, 10 pp.; The Friendly Side of Charity Organization, by Rev. E. Winchester Donald, D.D., 5 pp.; How Charity Organization helps the Pastors, by Rev. George Alexander, D.D., 4 pp.; The Personal Element in Charity, by Rev. Alexander Mackay-Smith, D.D., 9 pp.; The Need of Nerve in Charity, reprint from Charity Organization Reporter of London, 4 pp.; Economic and Moral Effects of Public Outdoor Relief, by Mrs. C. R. Lowell, 11 pp.; The Reform of Charity, by W. M. Salter, 8 pp., Handbook for Friendly Visitors, 88 pp., 16mo, paper 35 cents, cloth 50 cents.

PHILADELPHIA.

Manual and Directory of Charities, 1879, 217 pp.; Monthly Register, large quarto, 8 pp., now in its fourteenth year; Organization of Charity in Philadelphia, by D. O. Kellogg, 16 pp.; Suggestions to Ward Visitors, by Mrs. J. P. Lesley, 24 pp.; The Philadelphia Society for Organizing Charity, by Rev. W. H. Hodge ; a number of papers and essays now out of print.

PORTLAND, OREGON.

Facts of Interest to You concerning the City Board of Charities.

SAN FRANCISCO.

Monthly Circular of Information; various short papers.

Also, The Annual Reports of all the Charity Organization Societies in all the leading cities and towns named in Appendix A.

Appendix L.— *Concluded.*

The following, although not published by any of the Charity Organization Societies, are much used and circulated among them : —

Annual Reports of the National Conferences of Charities and Correction ; Annual Reports of the State Boards of Charities of the several States ; Charity Organization Review of the London C.O.S., monthly ; Children of the Poor, by Jacob A. Riis (Scribner), 300 pp. ; Dangerous Classes of New York, by Charles L. Brace, 1872, 468 pp.; Edward Denison, M.P., Letters, and Other Writings, by Sir Baldwyn Leighton, 12mo, 303 pp., paper (Scribner); How to help the Poor, by Mrs. James T. Fields, 125 pp. (Houghton, Mifflin & Co.); How the Other Half lives, by Jacob A. Riis (Scribner), 304 pp.; Improved Dwellings for the Laboring Classes, by Alfred T. White, 45 pp.; The Jukes, by R. S. Dugdale, 120 pp. (Putnam); Lend-a-Hand, Monthly Magazine, by Rev. E. E. Hale, D.D., Boston; Outdoor Relief and Tramps, by Professor Francis Wayland (New Haven); Public Relief and Private Charity, by Mrs. C. R. Lowell, 111 pp. (Putnam); Report on Care of Dependent Children in New York, by Mrs. Charles R. Lowell, Commissioner New York State Board of Charities, 77 pp.; Report on Outdoor Relief, by the same, 19 pp.; Report on the Workhouse, New York City, by the same, 15 pp.

APPENDIX M.

NECROLOGICAL.

BOSTON.

Rt. Rev. Phillips Brooks, D.D., Mrs. James Lodge, Miss Mary Anne Wales. (Enriched from their estates) Sidney Bartlett, Moses Day, J. W. Estabrooks, Mrs. Catharine C. Humphreys, Mrs. Mary M. McGregor.

BROOKLYN.

Charles Pratt, George B. Buzelle.

INDIANAPOLIS.

Rev. Oscar C. McCulloch.

NEW HAVEN.

Ex-Governor Hobart B. Bigelow, Thomas P. Gibbons, Mrs. Walter Osborn, Samuel G. Thorn, Samuel P. Wurts. (Enriched by their estates) Joshua Coit, Matthew G. Elliott.

NEW YORK.

Mrs. John Jacob Astor, Edgar S. Auchincloss, Jabez A. Bostwick, Benjamin G. Clark, Mrs. Cornelius Du Bois, Henry G. De Forest, Sidney Dillon, George B. Grinnell, Walter Hamlin, Rev. A. B. Hart, D.D., Robert B. Minturn, Cadwalader E. Ogden, Frederick Prime, Alfred Roosevelt, C. V. S. Roosevelt, Charles D. Scudder, M.D., John H. Sherwood, Lucius Tuckerman, S. O. Vander Poel, M.D., Julius Wadsworth, Robert Winthrop, Rev. Curtiss T. Woodruff. (Enriched from their estates or by memorial funds) Miss Leonora S. Bolles, William Smith Brown, Hector C. Havemeyer, Colles Johnston, Rev. C. W. Morrill, Mrs. Charles H. Rogers, Benjamin Stern, Adam W. Spies, Sidney Speyer, Mrs. Elijah Ward, Charles F. Woerishoffer.

PHILADELPHIA.

H. Lenox Hodge, M.D.

SYRACUSE.

Mrs. Harriet A. Dunlap, Mrs. Sarah Judson, Rev. Ovid Miner.